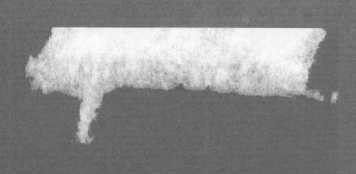

B2

The Visit

John Paul II in Ireland

A Historical Record

Veritas / A.C.W.

Dublin   1979

First published 1979 by
Veritas Publications,
7 & 8 Lower Abbey Street, Dublin 1,
and
A. C. W. Art Publishers Ltd,
57 Botanic Road, Dublin 9.

Compilation copyright © 1979 Veritas Publications and A.C.W. Art Publishers Ltd

Design by Jan de Fouw

Photography by: Fr Pat Cassells; Peter Devlin; Manuela Dumay, Paris; Felici, Rome; Ray Flynn; Green Studio Ltd; Kelly-Daly; Lensmen Ltd; Arturo Mari, Rome; Ray McManus; Network; Radio Telefís Éireann. Acknowledgements are also due to the Cultural Relations Committee of the Department of Foreign Affairs, The Mercier Press, the Board of Trinity College, Dublin.

Acknowledgements
The Publishers wish to acknowledge the cooperation of The Catholic Press and Information Office, Dublin, and Mgr Michael Olden, Maynooth, for "The Catholic Church in Ireland"; the Archbishop of Dublin for "Dublin Diocese" and "Phoenix Park"; Dr Peter Harbison for "Clonmacnois"; Rev. Réamonn Ó Muirí for "Armagh"; Catherine Rynne for "Knock": Rev. Martin Coen for "Galway"; Rev. Mark Tierney OSB for "Limerick"; Henry Boylan, and Gill and Macmillan for "Oliver Plunkett" from *Dictionary of Irish Biography*. Statistical information was supplied by: Archbishop's House, Dublin; Bishop's House, Galway; Bishop's House, Limerick; Bishop's House, Longford; President's Office, Maynooth; Mgr Horan, Knock; Parochial House, Drogheda.

ISBN 0 905092 97 X

Typeset by Joe Healy Typesetting, Dublin 2.
Origination and platemaking by Scanlith Services Ltd, Dublin 11.
Paper supplied by W. M. Papers Ltd, Dublin 9.
Printed in the Republic of Ireland by Dakota Ltd, Dublin 7,
and bound by John F. Newman & Son, Dublin 1.

Contents

Foreword by Tomás Cardinal Ó Fiaich

"I never felt closer to God than when I saw the Sacred Host raised by Pope John Paul in the Park on Saturday", said the white-haired lady beside me in the newsagent's. Despite her eighty-two years she had walked five miles to the Phoenix Park and five miles home again, quietly praying along the way, fingering the rosary she had received from the Holy Land as a child.

She was typical of the hundreds of thousands who prayed with the Holy Father at all his Irish stopping-points. With endless patience and infectious good humour, with the excitement of an All-Ireland Final, the fervour of the 1932 Eucharistic Congress, the pageantry of the Horse Show, the night-vigils of Lough Derg, the warmth of President Kennedy's welcome and the haunting melodies of a Fleadh Cheoil all rolled into one, the plain people of Ireland had taken over the country in a nationwide pilgrimage of prayer and self-sacrifice. Here with all their soul-stirring memories were the *cosmhuintir* of Irish tradition on the march, and true to their name they marched *de shiúl na gcos.*

Only those who lived through that unforgettable weekend can fully understand its impact. They can never hope to recapture in full its elusive atmosphere of spiritual joy and serenity, but this book will make its most precious moments come alive again. It will also convey much of the spirit of this unique event in Irish history to those who were unable to be present. Its pictures recapture the colour and exuberance of the occasion, while its text reproduces faithfully all the Holy Father's homilies and addresses in Ireland.

And what a wealth of teaching they embrace, all wrapped up in an Irish setting and applied to the contemporary Irish scene; a new *Book of Kells,* with Christ's gospel copied afresh in Gaelic script, illuminated by the hand of a master-craftsman and set off in a twentieth-century *cumhdach.*

Basically, of course, they contain only one message — God's love for us through Jesus Christ — preached over and over again with freshness, simplicity and sincerity. From that central theme came the eucharistic message of Dublin and the plea for peace, justice and reconciliation at Drogheda. In Galway it surged into a crescendo of love:

> **Críost liom,**
> **Críost romham,**
> **Críost 'mo dhiaidh.**

and in Cnoc Mhuire it flowed into a prayer for Mary's intercession:

> **A Mhuire na ngrás,**
> **A Mháthair Mhic Dé,**
> **Go gcuire tú**
> **Ar mo leas mé.**

The Irish people's response to God's loving message was highlighted at Maynooth — for the clergy and religious; and at Limerick — for the laity in their everyday lives. Everywhere it was a message of joy and peace — the Good News of Christ, which banishes sadness and gloom for ever:

> **Slán go deo le brón is buairt.**

Go gcuire an leabhar seo an t-aoibhneas céanna ar gach léitheoir.

✱ Tomás Cairdinéal Ó Fiaich

Ardeaspag Ard Mhacha

+ Tomáš Ó Fiaich

Ireland responds to Pope John Paul

A Pastoral Letter from the Archbishops and Bishops of Ireland

We wrote a Pastoral Letter to the Catholic people of Ireland on 2 September last, because we wanted to share with you our joy at the coming visit of Pope John Paul and to ask you to join in a programme of spiritual preparation for the visit and to give the Holy Father a "historic welcome" when he came. We write now to thank you for responding in a degree which far surpassed all predictions. Above all, we ask you to join with us in thanking God for the immense grace and love and happiness brought to Ireland by Pope John Paul.

John Paul our Pope

We thank God especially for Pope John Paul himself. Surely no visitor to our shores has ever done as much for our country as the Holy Father did in his three days amongst us. His obvious affection for Ireland, his veneration for our tradition, the tribute he paid to our national language by his own use of it, his accurate knowledge of the realities and the problems of contemporary Ireland, his deep concern for peace in our country, his confidence in our future, all have touched the "deep heart's core" of the men and women of Ireland, at home or in exile. From now on, he is not a distant holder of the most exalted office in the Church. He is one who walked amongst us, radiating love for all, reluctant to tear himself away from people, lonely at leaving us, and leaving us lonely as he went. In a new way, he is and will always be "John Paul *our* Pope". He is the Pope of our young people and adults, of parents and families, of our sick and our aged, of Irish mothers and babies, of our laity, our priests, our religious, our seminarists. From now on, there is a new meaning for all of us in the prayer of the Mass: "Make us grow in love together with John Paul, our Pope . . ." There will be more fervour in our prayer: "Strengthen in faith and love your pilgrim Church on earth, your servant, Pope John Paul, and all the Bishops . . ."

The people's welcome

Very many people share the credit for the success of the visit. Praise and gratitude are due to the priests, who worked so enthusiastically in the programme of spiritual preparation and who brought so much energy and talent to bear upon every facet of the complex organisation of the visit. We have already expressed our deep gratitude to all those lay persons and groups who worked with us with such dedication and such efficiency in the whole complex planning and organisation of the Papal visit. Their achievement has brought honour to Ireland in the eyes of a watching and admiring world. No thanks or praise would be enough for their contribution.

Yet, the real heroes of the hour, the true architects of the success of the visit, were the people themselves. Before the visit, we wrote: "We know that hundreds of thousands of Irish people will respond to the Pope's invitation. They will brave all obstacles and make all sacrifices to come into the presence of the Holy Father at one or other of the public ceremonies during his visit." Our words proved true beyond all expectations. Ireland for those unforgettable days was like a nation on pilgrimage, a whole pilgrim, praying people, on the march. The patience, the cheerfulness, the concern for others, the unity and love which filled the air were such as no one had ever experienced before. Pope John Paul reminded priests: "You are privileged to be pastors of a faithful people." We bishops have still greater reason to appreciate our privilege in being called to serve such a people. It is with new courage and confidence that we now resume, together with our priests, our task of sharing Christ's truth and love and forgiveness with you, in union with John Paul, our Pope. We do not forget the Christians of other Churches who generously shared with us in prayer and Christian fellowship during the time of the Pope's visit.

The prayerful preparation

The visit of Pope John Paul was an outpouring of grace such as could never result from human effort, but could only come from God. It was no feat of organisation which secured it, but the mighty movement of prayer which marked the weeks leading up to the visit. We had asked all to be involved in that prayer. Your response was overwhelming. Ireland in those weeks was a people at prayer, a "nation on retreat". Your prayers did more than our planning to make the visit a unique success. We asked you to pray:

> Let your Spirit descend, O Lord.
> Let your Spirit descend,
> and renew the face of the earth,
> and the face of this land.

The only explanation of the experience of the visit was that the Spirit of God did descend and pour out his gifts and his fruits over the people. If we sought to describe the atmosphere of the crowds during those days, the words which would come spontaneously to mind would be "love, joy, peace, patience, kindness, goodness, trustfulness, gentleness and self-control". Now these are precisely the "fruits of the Spirit", as enumerated by St Paul (Galatians 5:22). What we saw and heard was indeed, as at Pentecost, "the outpouring of that Spirit" (Acts 2:33).

Renew the face of this land

The task for all of us now is to ensure that the Papal visit is not just a passing emotional experience, soon to be only a memory. We must make it a continuing resource on which we draw for inspiration and strength for the decades ahead. We must be challenged by the Pope's visit, his example and his teaching to "go forth" as he said in Limerick, "go forth in the power of the Spirit to continue Christ's work and to follow his footsteps towards the end of the millenium, into the twenty-first century". This is a task for the whole Irish Church, not for bishops and priests alone, but for lay people too. As the Pope said: "Every lay Christian is an extraordinary work of God's grace and is called to the heights of holiness." During the preparations for the visit, we bishops worked side by side with lay people and received new and inspiring evidence of their depth of faith, their love of the Church, their dedication and their professional competence. We hope to go on working with them and benefitting from the experience, insights and skills of lay people, as together we try to serve the same Lord; for he works in all sorts of different ways in different people, but is the same God working in all of them (cf 1 Corinthians 12:3-7). He makes us all, bishops, priests, religious and laity, one body, in which each part must be equally concerned for all the others (cf 1 Corinthians 12:25).

The Holy Father's message ,

Pope John Paul did not set out to flatter us during his visit. It was no fantasy picture of an idealised and romantic Ireland from which he drew his words. He is aware of the problems and the dangers facing us. He warned us against complacency. "Be awake to all the dangers", he said to the priests; "stay firm in the faith; be brave and be strong". He challenged us all — bishops, priests, religious, seminarists, parents and youth, politicians, media. The important thing is that we listen to his message, accept it, put it into practice. Already some are selecting the passages they like — and usually these are the passages that affect others; and rejecting the passages they do not like — which usually are the passages calling for effort from themselves. Already some are explaining his message in ways which make him mean the opposite of what he said. The texts are there for all to have and study: please read these and judge the commentaries by the text. Cassettes of the Pope's actual voice are there for all to hear: please listen to the Pope before listening to the commentators.

The call to justice

On his first arrival in Ireland, the Pope announced himself as "a servant of Jesus Christ, a herald of his Gospel of justice and love". He challenged us all to examine both our personal life-style and our social systems and institutions by the Gospel standards of love and justice. He declared that we cannot be Sunday Christians only; we must bring Christ into our "work, our commercial dealings, our trade union or employers' or professional meetings". He pointed to the danger of letting affluence breed grasping and aggressive attitudes, concerned about the interests of oneself and one's group, and uncaring about the poor and the weak. He reminded us of the challenge of poverty and deprivation, and of the need to create job opportunities, especially for the young. He stressed the social implications of the Gospel:

> Reaching the goals of justice in the economic and. social fields will require that religious convictions and fervour be not separated from a moral and social conscience, especially for those who plan and control the economic process, be they legislators, Government officials, industrialists, trade unionists, office workers or manual workers.

We shall not be responding adequately to the Pope's visit unless we now bring new vigour to the task of tackling the injustices in our society, so that there may be "consistency between what we believe and what we do".

A mission of peace and reconciliation

At Drogheda, Pope John Paul said he had come "on a great mission of peace and reconciliation".

From Drogheda, he appealed for an end to violence, for a determined political movement towards a just settlement of the conflict in Northern Ireland. He pleaded, on his knees, with the men and women engaged in violence "to turn away from the paths of violence". He pleaded with young people caught up in organisations engaged in violence, to seek justice instead by the ways of peace. In Drogheda and again in Galway, he asked young people to "form an interior judgement of conscience to determine where they, as young Catholics stand" on the matter of violence. He implored young people:

> I say to you, with all the love I have for you, with all the trust I have in young people; do not listen to voices which speak the language of hatred, revenge, retaliation . . . Live life, respect life, in yourselves and in others.

The Pope asked fathers and mothers to give an example to their children of love and forgiveness and not let even one child grow up with "nothing but the experience of violence and hate".

The Pope appealed to us all: "Do not believe in violence; do not support violence." This is a call to everyone to try to purge hatred and violence out of his or her emotions, attitudes and speech. It is above all a solemn call to everyone to refuse any voluntary support or cooperation to those planning or committing deeds of violence. We must not become guilty ourselves by sharing the guilt of another's sin of violence.

The Pope spoke with unprecedented firmness and force to "all who bear political responsibility for the affairs of Ireland", to "show that there is a peaceful, political way to justice". He spoke to Protestants, begging them never to think "that the Pope is an enemy, a danger or a threat", but instead to see in him "a friend and a brother in Christ".

May all those to whom the Pope spoke listen, reflect and act. May the paramilitary leaders, the politicians, the Governments, those responsible for law and order, the people of the Catholic community, the people of the Protestant community, may they seize this opportunity which the Pope's visit has given us to work for peace with consent, with honour, and with justice. We shall not have so favourable an opportunity offered to us again. It will be unforgiveable if we do not act, and act now. The judgement of history, the judgement of God, are upon us. Later on will be too late; and then we shall in bitter sorrow blame ourselves that we "did not recognise our opportunity when God offered it" (cf Luke 19:44).

Prayer is the key

The key to peace is prayer. The Pope called for a "great intense and growing prayer" by the whole Church. May the whole Church in Ireland be united in that prayer from the heart that God may send his peace to Ireland. Prayer is the key to the whole renewal of faith and Christian life in Ireland for which Pope John Paul appealed. Prayer was the secret of the spiritual and material success of his visit. May that prayer continue in the aftermath of the visit, so that the message which the Holy Father brought us from Christ may bear lasting fruit; and so that indeed, by God's grace, all things may be made new in our land.

We ask that the Feast of the Immaculate Conception of the Blessed Virgin Mary, 8 December, be observed in every parish as a day of special prayer. On that day, recalling the moving prayer of trust and dedication to Our Lady spoken by the Pope in the name of all of us in Knock, we shall join in nation-wide giving of thanks to God for the grace of the visit and in praying that that grace may act as a leaven transforming the whole life of our country.

Special meeting of bishops

In order to reflect deeply on the Holy Father's message and to join an organised and wide-ranging response to it, we the bishops intend to come together again for a special meeting in December. We ask for your prayers that this meeting may be successful in working out a programme of pastoral action which may enable all sectors and age groups in the Church to respond worthily to the message for Ireland of the Pope who came to us "as a servant of Jesus Christ, a herald of his gospel of justice and love, as Bishop of Rome, as successor of the Apostle Peter."

Praised be Jesus Christ.
Moladh go deo le Dia.

On behalf of the Hierarchy of Ireland,

✠ Tomás Cardinal Ó Fiaich,
Archbishop of Armagh

✠ Dermot Ryan,
Archbishop of Dublin

✠ Thomas Morris,
Archbishop of Cashel

✠ Joseph Cunnane,
Archbishop of Tuam

"Moladh go deo le Dia!"

Address on arrival at Dublin Airport

"It is with immense joy . . . that I set foot today on Irish soil."

It is with immense joy and with profound gratitude to the most Holy Trinity that I set foot today on Irish soil.

Moladh go deo le Dia!

I come to you as a servant of Jesus Christ, a herald of his Gospel of justice and love, as Bishop of Rome, as successor of the Apostle Peter, and in the words of Peter I offer you the greeting of my heart: "Peace to all of you who are in Christ" (1 Pet 5:14).

I deeply appreciate the welcome of His Excellency the President of Ireland who, as the representative of all upright citizens, extends to me the warm hospitality of this land.

I am grateful moreover to my brothers in the episcopate, who are here to greet me in the name of the whole Church in Ireland, that I love so much. I am very happy to walk among you — in the footsteps of Saint Patrick and in the path of the Gospel that he left you as a great heritage — being convinced that Christ is here: "Christ before me, Christ behind me . . . Christ in the heart of every man who thinks of me, Christ in the mouth of every man who speaks of me."

At this moment of my arrival I feel the need to express my esteem for the Christian traditions of this land, as well as the gratitude of the Catholic Church for the glorious contribution made by Ireland over the centuries to the spreading of the faith. From this capital city I send my greetings to all the Irish throughout the world.

And as I invoke God's blessings on Ireland, I commend all her people to the prayers of Our Blessed Lady, to the intercession of Mary, Mother of Jesus and Queen of Peace, under whose patronage I place my pastoral visit.

Praised be Jesus Christ.

Moladh go deo le Dia!

hgeneratio

The Catholic Church in Ireland

Early Irish Christianity

The year A.D. 432 is generally recognised as the year in which St Patrick, the main evangelist of pagan Ireland, arrived in the country. There is little doubt that Ireland had come under some Christian influence before that date; its proximity to Britain would have made that inevitable. But Patrick remains the man who established Christianity in the country and set up the basic ecclesiastical organisation of the early Irish Church.

The early Irish Church, as was the practice elsewhere, had its bishops and priests who, following Patrick, converted the population to the faith in a remarkably short time. A few years after Patrick's arrival Ireland was Christian.

An interesting feature of the early Irish Church was that it very quickly became monastic. Groups of priests came together all over the country in primitive monastic settlements and, within a brief period of time, the monasteries were the organisational centre of the Church in Ireland. The bishop was frequently a member of the monastic community, not necessarily the head of it. Ireland was to wait many centuries before a diocesan system was established.

The monasteries were many and they thrived. Even today, in many parts of the country, the remains of these early foundations still exist, e.g. Clonmacnois. They became cultural as well as religious centres. Works of art in stone and script were created within them: the high crosses, the beautiful books such as the *Book of Kells* and the *Book of Durrow,* are clear witness to the high culture which developed in monastic Ireland.

The monasteries were also the power-houses from which there developed a remarkable missionary thrust — a development which occurred within a century of Patrick's time. In the sixth century Irish monks left Ireland and established monasteries in other countries. Beginning with the northern islands such as the Orkneys, they established settlements in Scotland where Iona, founded by St Columcille, was to be a powerful centre of evangelisation. They swept through a European continent which had been ravaged and impoverished after the fall of the Roman Empire.

The sixth and seventh centuries saw Irish missionaries exercising enormous influence on religion and culture in France, Germany, Switzerland, Italy. There were St Columbanus in the Vosges mountains and his famous monastery in Bobbio in northern Italy, St Gall in Switzerland, St Kilian in Wurzburg, and St Virgilius in Salzburg. The number of men and of monasteries was vast; their influence on a declining Europe was remarkable. For the Irish Church the period between St Patrick and the year A.D. 800 was a golden age.

The medieval Irish Church

Around the year A.D. 800 things began to happen which were to put an end to the golden age of the Irish Church and create much upheaval in the country. During the ninth century raids by invaders from Norway, Denmark and Sweden on Irish monasteries were incessant. Works of art were stolen; monasteries were razed to the ground. The monks held out as best they could: some of the still standing round towers were built often as defence against the invaders from the north. But a very unsettled period descended on the Irish Church for three centuries after the Viking invasions, and in the twelfth century there took place in Ireland what was already occurring in Europe — a much needed reform of the Church.

A very important figure in this reform was St Malachy, Archbishop of Armagh (1095-1148) who was a close associate and friend of the great European reformer, St Bernard of Clairvaux. But there were many others. Out of the twelfth century came the firm establishment of dioceses as we now know them in Ireland, and the establishment of new and great monasteries — Cistercian, Augustinian and others.

In the very century in which Church reform was taking place another and more lasting invasion of the century began — the Normans had conquered England, and in 1169 they set foot in Ireland. From that date what might loosely be called the English invasion of Ireland began. Political and religious divisions became intertwined very quickly; in religion there were native and English (or Norman) sections; in politics there were native and English (or Norman) allegiances. Division and tension continued within the Irish Church from the twelfth century right up to the Reformation in the sixteenth century. When England became Protestant in the sixteenth century Ireland remained Catholic. The Reformation increased tension between the Irish and the English and further fuelled the troubles which beset Ireland to this day.

After the Reformation

In the centuries after the Reformation, Ireland was increasingly viewed by England as a source of threat and rebellion. It was staunchly Catholic; it was in communication with Catholic powers in Europe — the Papacy, France and Spain. During the seventeenth and eighteenth centuries persecution of the Irish was more or less constant. The English also engaged in a policy of plantation — that is, introducing loyal subjects from England and Scotland who were given large tracts of land in Ireland. This plantation was particularly successful in Ulster and from it stems much of the division which is present between different sections in that province today.

In particular, the eighteenth century marked the period of the Penal Laws by which Catholics were deprived of any political rights. During this period, some thirty Irish colleges were established on the European mainland, extending from Lisbon to Prague. The most important of these was Collège des Irlandais, Paris, now a Polish seminary, where John Paul II spent some time as a priest-student. The Irish had espoused the cause of the House of Stuart, rival claimant to the throne of England and Catholic in religion. It was only after a series of clear defeats of the Stuarts that the threat was removed and the English Parliament began to grant concessions to Catholics.

Before and after 1800 rights were conceded to Catholics in Ireland. Permission was given for seminaries to be established for the education of priests. The most important of these was Maynooth College which was founded in 1795.

The nineteenth century was a period of great growth for the Irish Church. Persecution was over, and the Church was given a chance to develop, organisationally and devotionally. As in the early period of the sixth and seventh centuries the happy home situation produced a strong missionary thrust. Irish men and women went as missionaries to every part of the English-speaking world and to Africa, India and China. They followed their people who were forced to leave Ireland because of the poverty and terrible famines which were a prevalent feature of the nineteenth century.

During those years the Irish Church became highly organised: schools, religious orders, lay societies were established and flourished. Contact with Rome was intimate and powerful. The Church was free from many of the difficulties which had hindered it for centuries.

The Church in modern times

When the twenty-six counties which now form the Republic of Ireland broke with Britain in 1922 and Ireland was partitioned, the Catholic Church — like the other Christian Churches — continued to be organised as a single ecclesiastical unit. It is composed of four archdioceses, each with an archbishop — Armagh (north), Dublin (east), Cashel (south) and Tuam (west) and twenty-six dioceses. Dioceses range in population from nearly a million in Dublin to about 33,000 in the south Midlands diocese of Clonfert.

Armagh, the historic seat of St Patrick, is the "ecclesiastical capital of Ireland". Its archbishop — usually a cardinal — is the Primate of All Ireland, while the Archbishop of Dublin is the Primate of Ireland. These titles have nothing to do with modern Irish politics — they stem from a medieval dispute over primacy between Dublin and Armagh. Basically, the diocesan structure as it is today remained unchanged since the middle ages.

It is estimated that about 94 per cent of the population of the Republic (which stands at 3.3 million according to the latest census) is Catholic while in Northern Ireland about 31 per cent of the population of one million is Catholic.

The country has 1,298 parishes served by about 4000 priests. Parishes range in population from over 20,000 in some Dublin suburbs to about a tenth of that number in some rural areas. The population of the eastern seaboard has been growing at an enormous rate and this has imposed heavy demands in servicing the needs of the Church in terms of churches and schools in the rapidly developing suburbs of Dublin.

In the past fifteen years, since 1964, the number of parishes in the diocese has almost doubled. But with the growth in population and the decline in emigration from Ireland, many other dioceses are also developing rapidly, particularly Cork, Galway, Limerick and Waterford.

The influence of the Irish on the development of the Catholic Church abroad, particularly in the English-speaking world, has been enormous. Emigration was one of the most striking features of modern Irish history and Ireland is today one of the few countries in the world with a lower population than it had 150 years ago. The millions who went abroad over the years were followed by thousands of priests, nuns and brothers to serve their spiritual and educational needs. But it was not only to the Irish abroad that priests and religious went, they also went as missionaries to every continent.

Today there are 5,613 Irish missionaries working in eighty-six different countries throughout Africa, Asia, Central and South America and Oceania. Almost two-thirds of the number are in Africa with the largest concentrations in South Africa (987), Nigeria (770), Kenya (574) and Zambia (389). There are 1,258 in Asia including 294 in Hong Kong and 291 in the Philippine Islands. Six hundred work in Latin America with the biggest number in Brazil (176).

These numbers have changed little in the past ten years though the number of brothers has diminished slightly while the number of lay missionaries has increased by a third (from 222 to 317).

The Catholic Church in Ireland faces immense challenges as it approaches the end of the second millennium. While the rate of religious practice is still one of the highest in the world (around 91 per cent of the Catholic population were found to attend Mass at least weekly in a major survey carried out in the Republic in 1973-1974), there has been evidence of some decline among the younger age groups. The 1973-1974 survey was carried out on behalf of the bishops, partly as an aid to pastoral planning for the future. While it revealed many encouraging features about the Church in Ireland it showed that there are many areas where the task of the Church is urgent. For example, the survey also revealed that of the 91 per cent only 28 per cent received Holy Communion each week and this raises questions about the quality of people's participation at Mass.

The same survey showed that living a happy family life was a very important goal of a large majority of Catholics living in the Irish Republic.

A similar survey of university students conducted in 1976 showed that 70 per cent of students brought up as Catholics go to Mass once a week and 20 per cent go more often. But it also revealed that 14 per cent no longer regarded themselves as Catholics.

The number of religious in Ireland is relatively large, with around 13,700 nuns. However, both the nuns and the brothers (now around 2,000) have been severely affected by the decline in vocations to the religious life.

The Church is closely involved in the provision of health care in Ireland, with religious orders running hospitals and clinics. Many of these were started as a service to the poor, and now there is cooperation between the religious and the State in continuing to provide care under the State's social welfare service.

Collège des Irlandais

Phoenix Park

The Archdiocese of Dublin

The Diocese of Dublin is believed to have been first organised in 1034, with the consecration of Bishop Dunan, shortly after a pilgrimage to Rome by Sitric, Norse King of Dublin.

Dunan was succeeded in 1074 by Bishop Patrick, who was known as Primas Hiberniae (Primate of Ireland). He was followed by Bishop Donngus in 1085 and Bishop Samuel in 1096. Samuel was consecrated by St Anselm of Canterbury at Winchester, and his tomb is in St Michan's.

In 1121, a deacon named Gregory was appointed bishop. He was a strong leader, bringing Dublin into the twelfth century reform. At the Synod of Kells he was appointed archbishop, the first in the diocese. The most celebrated Archbishop of Dublin was St Laurence O'Toole (1162-1180). The eighth centenary of his death will be celebrated in 1980.

The Wellington Monument

Phoenix Park

The Phoenix Park (Páirc an Fhionn Uisce) was first enclosed in 1662. At an early stage it comprised over 2,000 acres and extended beyond the Liffey to the south. In 1680 the lands south of the Chapelizod road were excluded. This, and later minor alterations, reduced the Park to its present area of 1,752 acres. Phoenix House, which gave its name to the Park, stood on St Thomas' Hill near the present Islandbridge Gate.

Most of the Park, which is the largest enclosed one in Europe, is open to the public. Within it are several noteworthy buildings. Áras an Uachtaráin, the residence of the President of Ireland, dates from 1750 and served from 1782 to 1922 as the residence of the British viceroys. The former Apostolic Nunciature, earlier the Under Secretary's Lodge, stands on the site of Ashtown Castle on lands once the property of the Priory of St John without Newgate. The United States Ambassador's residence, built in 1774, in former times was the Chief Secretary's Lodge. The Ordnance Survey Offices include Mountjoy House built about 1728. St Mary's Chest Hospital was formerly the Hibernian Military School dating from 1766.

Within the Phoenix Park are the extensive Dublin Zoological Gardens and the ornamental grounds known as the Peoples' Gardens. There are numerous sports fields for hurling, camogie, football, cricket, and polo.

West of St Mary's Chest Hospital, on the hill of Knockmary, stands a prehistoric burial chamber of the early bronze age. The tumulus which covered it was opened in 1838 and skeletons, pottery and other relics, now in the National Museum were discovered. A similar sepulchre found in a gravel pit at Chapelizod is re-erected in the Zoological Gardens.

Phoenix Park
    Attendance: 1,250,000
    Concelebrants: 155 (124 bishops, 31 priests)
    Communion priests: 2,000
    Communicants: 750,000 approx.
    Choir: 6,000
    Stewards: 15,000
    Deaths: 0
    Births: 2
    Gifts offered: sheaves of wheat, loaves of bread

Homily during Mass at the Phoenix Park

"The bishop comes among the laity as one who serves."

"I have come to you as Bishop of Rome."

A phobail dhílis na hÉireann!
Dear brothers and sisters in Jesus Christ,
1.   Like Saint Patrick, I too have heard "the voice of the Irish" calling to me, and so I have come to you, to all of you in Ireland.

From the very beginning of its faith, Ireland has been linked with the Apostolic See of Rome. The early records attest that your first bishop, Palladius, was sent to Ireland by Pope Celestine and that Saint Patrick, who succeeded Palladius, was "confirmed in the faith" by Pope Leo the Great. Among the sayings attributed to Patrick is the famous one addressed to the "Church of the Irish, nay of the Romans", showing them how they must pray in order to be "Christians as the Romans are".

This union of charity between Ireland and the Holy Roman Church has remained inviolable and unbreakable down all the centuries. You Irish Catholics have kept and loved the unity and peace of the Catholic Church, treasuring it above all earthly treasure. Your people have spread this love for the Catholic Church everywhere they went, in every century of your history. This has been done by the earliest monks and the missionaries of Europe's dark ages, by the refugees from persecution, by the exiles and by the missionaries — men and women — of the last century and this one.

I have come to you as Bishop of Rome and pastor of the whole Church in order to celebrate this union with you in the sacrifice of the Eucharist, here in Ireland's capital city of Dublin, for the first time in Irish history. As I stand at this moment, a pilgrim for Christ to the land from which so many pilgrims for Christ, *peregrini pro Christo,* went out over Europe, the Americas, Australia, Africa, Asia, I am living a moment of intense emotion. As I stand here, in the company of so many hundreds of thousands of Irish men and women, I am thinking of how many times, across how many centuries, the Eucharist has been celebrated in this land. How many and how varied the places where Mass has been offered — in stately medieval and in splendid modern cathedrals; in early monastic and in modern churches; at Mass rocks in the glens and forests by "hunted priests" and in poor thatch-covered chapels, for a people poor in worldly goods but rich in the things of the spirit; in "wake-houses" or "station houses", or at great open-air hostings of the faithful — on the top of Croagh Patrick and at Lough Derg. Small matter where the Mass was offered. For the Irish, it was always the Mass that mattered. How many have found in it the spiritual strength to live, even through the times of greatest hardship and poverty, through days of persecutions and vexations — dear brothers and sisters, dear sons and daughters of Ireland, permit me, together with you, to glance back over your history, in the light of the Eucharist celebrated here for so many centuries.

2.   From the upper room in Jerusalem, from the last supper, in a certain sense, the Eucharist writes the history of human hearts and of human communities. Let us reflect on all those, who, being nourished on the body and blood of the Lord, have lived and died on this island, bearing in themselves, because of the Eucharist, the pledge of eternal life. Let us think of so many generations of sons and daughters

of this country, and at the same time, sons and daughters of the Church. May this Eucharist of ours be celebrated in the atmosphere of the great communion of the saints. We form a spiritual union in this Mass with all the generations who have done God's will throughout the ages up to the present day. We are one in faith and spirit with the vast throng which filled this Phoenix Park on the occasion of the last great Eucharistic hosting held on this spot, at the Eucharistic Congress in 1932.

Faith in Christ has profoundly penetrated into the consciousness and life of your ancestors. The Eucharist transformed their souls for eternal life, in union with the living God. May this exceptional Eucharistic encounter of today be at the same time a prayer for the dead, for your ancestors and forebears. With their help, may it become more fruitfully a prayer for the living, for the present generation of sons and daughters of today's Ireland, preparing for the end of the twentieth century, so that they can meet the challenges that will be put before them.

3.   Yes, Ireland, that has overcome so many difficult moments in her history, is being challenged in a new way today, for she is not immune from the influence of ideologies and trends which present-day civilisation and progress carry with them. The very capability of mass media to bring the whole world into your homes produces a new kind of confrontation with values and trends that up until now have been alien to Irish society. Pervading materialism imposes its dominion on man today in many different forms and with an aggressiveness that spares no one. The most sacred principles, which were the sure guides for the behaviour of individuals and society, are being hollowed out by false pretences concerning freedom, the sacredness of life, the indissolubility of marriage, the true sense of human sexuality, the right attitude towards the material goods that progress has to offer. Many people now are tempted to self-indulgence and consumerism, and human identity is often defined by what one owns. Prosperity and affluence, even when they are only beginning to be available to larger strata of society, tend to make people assume that they have a right to all that prosperity can bring, and thus they can become more selfish in their demands. Everybody wants a full freedom in all the areas of human behaviour and new models of morality are being proposed in the name of would-be freedom. When the moral fibre of a nation is weakened, when the sense of personal responsibility is diminished, then the door is open for the justification of injustice, for violence in all its forms, and for the manipulation of the many by the few. The challenge that is already with us is the temptation to accept as true freedom what in reality is only a new form of slavery.

4.   And so, it becomes all the more urgent to steep ourselves in the truth that comes from Christ, "who is the way, the truth and the life" (Jn 14:6), and in the strength that he himself offers us through his spirit. It is especially in the Eucharist that the power and the love of the Lord are given to us.

The sacrifice of the body and blood of Jesus Christ offered up for us is an act of supreme love on the part of the Saviour. It is his great victory over sin and death — a victory that he communicates to us. The Eucharist is a promise of eternal life, since Jesus himself tells us: "He who eats my flesh and drinks my blood has eternal life, and I will raise him up at the last day" (Jn 6:54).

The holy sacrifice of the Mass is meant to be the festive celebration of our salvation. In the Mass we give thanks and praise to God our Father for having given us the redemption through the precious blood of Jesus Christ. The Eucharist is also the centre of the Church's unity, as well as her greatest treasure. In the words of the Second Vatican Council, the Eucharist contains "the Church's entire spiritual wealth" (*Presbyterorum Ordinis*, 5).

"I am the Living Bread which has come down from Heaven."

Today I wish to express the gratitude of Jesus Christ and his Church for the devotion that Ireland has shown to the holy Eucharist. As successor of Peter and Vicar of Christ, I assure you that the Mass is indeed the source and summit of our Christian life.

On Sunday mornings in Ireland, no one seeing the great crowds making their way to and from Mass could have any doubt about Ireland's devotion to the Mass. For them a whole Catholic people is seen to be faithful to the Lord's command: "Do this in memory of me." May the Irish Sunday continue always to be the day when the whole people of God — the "pobal Dé" — makes its way to the house of God, which the Irish call the house of the people — the "Teach an Phobail". I have learned with great joy that large numbers also come to Mass several times each week and even every day. This practice is a great source of grace and of growth in holiness.

5.   Yes, it is from the Eucharist that all of us receive the grace and strength for daily living — to live real Christian lives, in the joy of knowing that God loves us, that Christ died for us, and that the Holy Spirit lives in us.

Our full participation in the Eucharist is the real source of the Christian spirit that we wish to see in our personal lives and in all aspects of society. Whether we serve in politics, in the economic, cultural, social or scientific fields — no matter what our occupation is — the Eucharist is a challenge to our daily lives.

Dear brothers and sisters! There must always be consistency between what we believe and what we do. We cannot live on the glories of our past Christian history. Our union with Christ in the Eucharist must be expressed in the truth of our lives today — in our actions, in our behaviour, in our life-style, and in our relationships with others. For each one of us the Eucharist is a call to ever greater effort, so that we may live as true followers of Jesus: truthful in our speech, generous in our deeds, concerned, respectful of the dignity and rights of all persons, whatever their rank or income, self-sacrificing, fair and just, kind, considerate, compassionate and self-controlled — looking to the well-being of our families, our young people, our country, Europe and the world. The truth of our union with Jesus Christ in the Eucharist is tested by whether or not we really love our fellow men and women; it is tested by how we treat others, especially our families: husbands and wives, children and parents, brothers and sisters. It is tested by whether or not we try to be reconciled with our enemies, on whether or not we forgive those who hurt us or offend us. It is tested by whether we practise in life what our faith teaches us. We must always remember what Jesus said: "You are my friends if you do what I command you" (Jn 15:14).

*"The Eucharist is the
real source of
the Christian spirit."*

6.   The Eucharist is also a great call to conversion. We know that it is an invitation to the banquet; that, by nourishing ourselves on the Eucharist, we receive in it the body and blood of Christ, under the appearances of bread and wine. Precisely because of this invitation, the Eucharist is and remains the call to conversion. If we receive it as such a call, such an invitation, it brings forth in us its proper fruits. It transforms our lives. It makes us a "new man", a "new creature" (cf Gal 6:15. Eph 2:15. 2 Cor 5: 17). It helps us not to be "overcome by evil, but to overcome evil by good" (cf Rom 12:21). The Eucharist helps love to triumph in us — love over hatred, zeal over indifference.

The call to conversion in the Eucharist links the Eucharist with that other great sacrament of God's love, which is penance. Every time that we receive the sacrament of penance or reconciliation, we receive the forgiveness of Christ, and we know that this forgiveness comes to us through the merits of his death — the very death that we celebrate in the Eucharist. In the sacrament of reconciliation, we are all invited to meet Christ personally in this way, and to do so frequently. This encounter with Jesus is so very important that I wrote in my first encyclical letter these words:

> In faithfully observing the centuries-old practice of the sacrament of penance – the practice of individual confession with a personal act of sorrow and the intention to amend and make satisfaction – the Church is therefore defending the human soul's individual right: man's right to a more personal encounter with the crucified forgiving Christ, with Christ saying, through the minister of the sacrament of reconciliation: "Your sins are forgiven; go, and do not sin again."

Because of Christ's love and mercy, there is no sin that is too great to be forgiven; there is no sinner who will be rejected. Every person who repents will be received by Jesus Christ with forgiveness and immense love.

It was with great joy that I received the news that the Irish bishops had asked all the faithful to go to confession as part of a great spiritual preparation for my visit to Ireland. You could not have given me a greater joy or a greater gift. And if today there is someone who is still hesitating, for one reason or another, please remember this: the person who knows how to acknowledge the truth of guilt, and asks Christ for forgiveness, enhances his own human dignity and manifests spiritual greatness.

I take this occasion to ask all of you to continue to hold this sacrament of penance in special honour, for ever. Let all of us remember the words of Pius XII in regard to frequent confession: "Not without the inspiration of the Holy Spirit was this practice introduced into the Church."

Dear brothers and sisters, the call to conversion and repentance comes from Christ, and always leads us back to Christ in the Eucharist.

I wish also at this time to recall to you an important truth affirmed by the Second Vatican Council, namely: "the spiritual life, nevertheless, is not confined to . . . participation in the liturgy" (*Sacrosanctum Concilium,* 12). And so I also encourage you in the other exercises of devotion that you have lovingly preserved for centuries, especially those in regard to the Blessed Sacrament. These acts of piety honour God and are useful for our Christian lives. They give joy to our hearts, and help us to appreciate more the liturgical worship of the Church.

The visit to the Blessed Sacrament — so much a part of Ireland, so much a part of your piety, so much a part of your pilgrimage to Knock — is a great treasure of the Catholic faith.

It nourishes social love and gives us opportunities for adoration and thanksgiving, for reparation and supplication.

"The Eucharist is also a great call to conversion."

D3728 3

Benediction of the Blessed Sacrament, exposition and adoration of the Blessed Sacrament, holy hours and Eucharistic processions are likewise precious elements of your heritage — in full accord with the teaching of the Second Vatican Council.

At this time, it is also my joy to reaffirm before Ireland and the whole world the wonderful teaching of the Catholic Church regarding Christ's consoling presence in the Blessed Sacrament: his real presence in the fullest sense; the substantial presence by which the whole and complete Christ, God and man, is present (cf *Mysterium Fidei,* 39). The Eucharist in the Mass and outside of the Mass, is the body and blood of Jesus Christ, and is therefore deserving of the worship that is given to the living God, and to him alone (cf *Mysterium Fidei,* 55; Paul VI, Address of 15 June 1978).

And so, dear brothers and sisters, every act of reverence, every genuflexion that you make before the Blessed Sacrament, is important because it is an act of faith in Christ, an act of love for Christ. And every sign of the cross and gesture of respect made each time you pass a church is also an act of faith.

May God preserve you in this faith — this holy Catholic faith — this faith in the Blessed Sacrament.

I end, dear brothers and sisters, beloved sons and daughters of Ireland, by recalling how divine providence has used this island on the edge of Europe for the conversion of the European continent, that continent which has been for two thousand years the continent of the first evangelisation. I myself am a son of that nation which received the Gospel more than a thousand years ago, many centuries later than your homeland. When in 1966, we solemnly recalled the millenium of the baptism of Poland, we

"Semper fidelis."

"I know from firsthand experience the value of the services you render . . ."

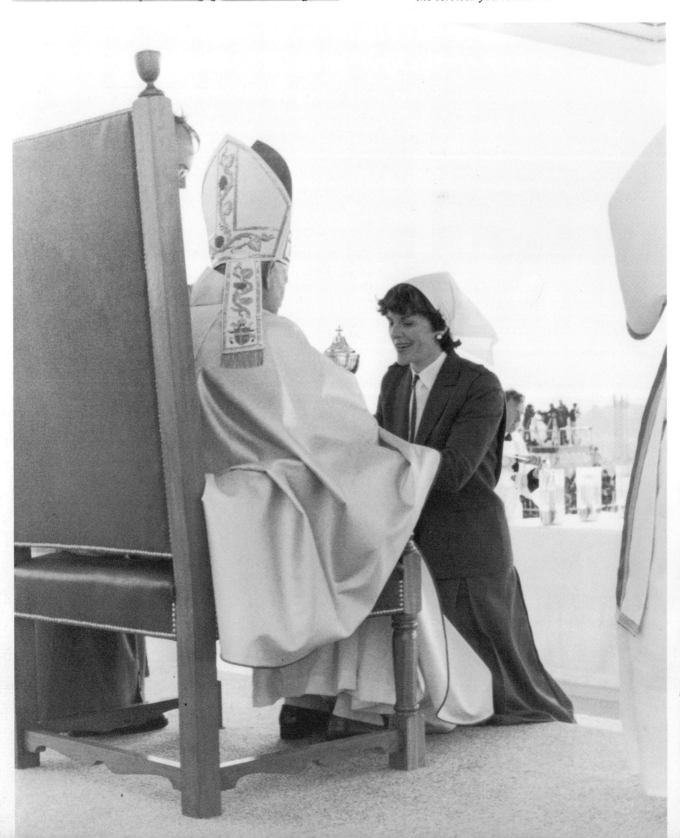

recalled with gratitude also those Irish missionaries who, among others, participated in the work of the first evangelisation of the country that extends east and west from the Vistula.

One of my closest friends, a famous professor of history in Cracow, having learned of my intention to visit Ireland, said: "What a blessing that the Pope goes to Ireland. This country deserves it in a special way." I, too, have always thought like this. Thus I thought that the centenary of the sanctuary of the Mother of God at Knock constitutes, this year, a providential occasion for the Pope's visit to Ireland. So, by this visit, I am expressing my sense of what Ireland "deserves", and also satisfying deep needs of my own heart.

I am paying a great debt to Jesus Christ, who is the Lord of history and the author of our salvation.

Hence I express my joy that I can be with you today, 29 September 1979, feast of Saint Michael, Saint Gabriel and Saint Raphael, archangels, and that I can celebrate the holy sacrifice of the Mass and give witness before you to Christ and to his paschal mystery. Thus I can proclaim the vivifying reality of conversion through the Eucharist and the sacrament of penance, in the midst of the present generation of the sons and daughters of Ireland. *Metanoeite,* "be converted" (Mk 1:15). Be converted every day, because constantly, every day, the kingdom of God draws closer. On the road of this temporal world, let Christ be the Lord of your souls, for eternal life. Amen.

"I too have heard 'the voice of the Irish'."

*Oliver Plunkett — contemporary portrait
by Garnet Morphey, National Gallery of Ireland*

Drogheda

The Archdiocese of Armagh

The Archdiocese of Armagh stretches from Lough Neagh in the north to the river Boyne in the south, straddling the Border and incorporating all of Co. Louth and substantial parts of counties Armagh, Tyrone and Derry. It takes its name, of course, from the city of Armagh, the ecclesiastical capital of Ireland or the "primatial city" as it is affectionately known by its inhabitants. It was already a place of importance when St Patrick chose it for his first church and became its first bishop.

Armagh is derived from the Irish Ard Mhacha, Macha's Height. Macha was a legendary queen who ruled there in pre-Christian times. A few miles to the west of the city are the remains of Emain Macha, so evocative of the great names of Irish history and saga: Cuchulainn, Fergus, Conor Mac Nessa and the heroes of the Red Branch. For centuries after St Patrick, Armagh was the centre of Christian learning. The magnificent *Book of Armagh*, a relic of its golden age, still survives. Today, two beautiful cathedrals on the city's two little central drumlin hills tower over its ancient winding concentric streets.

The Primate of all Ireland lives there: Cardinal Tomás Ó Fiaich, one hundredth and thirteenth successor in an unbroken line from Patrick, a line that is proud of two canonised saints, Malachy, a native of the city, who died in the arms of St Bernard, 2 November 1148, and Oliver Plunkett, the martyr bishop, who died 1 July 1681. St Patrick sowed the seed on the Hill of Macha. Pope John Paul II recognised the harvest of a long tradition when he paid tribute to Ireland's faith at Drogheda, 29 September 1979: "I seek first those places which carry in themselves the sign of the "beginning", and "beginning" is connected with "firstness", with primacy. Such a place on Irish soil is Armagh, for centuries the Episcopal See of the Primate of Ireland."

Saint Oliver Plunkett 1625-1681

Oliver Plunkett was born on 1 November 1625 at Loughcrew, Co. Meath, of a family closely related to the Earls of Fingall and Roscommon. In 1647 he went to Rome to study at the Irish College and was ordained in 1654. Remaining in Rome, he taught theology and became procurator, or representative, of the Irish bishops. When the See of Armagh became vacant in 1669, he was chosen to succeed and, having been consecrated archbishop (in Ghent, because of the penal laws), made his way to Dublin in 1670.

In poverty and hardship he laboured to re-organise his diocese, holding a provincial synod and confirming ten thousand people within three months. He established the Jesuits at Drogheda (where they opened a school and a seminary), strove to maintain discipline in his diocese after years of neglect and to restore good relations between the diocesan and religious clergy, and worked to prevent the infiltration of Jansenism from France.

After three years of comparative freedom from persecution, he was forced to go into hiding in 1673, and from then until his arrest in 1679 his life was one of continual danger and grinding physical hardship. The "Popish Plot" of Titus Oates caused panic in England in 1678 and the persecution in Ireland was intensified. An order of expulsion was made against all Catholic bishops and priests, and Plunkett was lodged in Dublin Castle in December 1679 on a charge of conspiring to bring about an armed rebellion. Only one witness, an apostate priest, could be found; the Archbishop was then removed to Newgate prison in London.

After months of delay, a travesty of a trial took place, and he was found guilty of high treason for alleged complicity in the Titus Oates plot. He was hanged, drawn and quartered at Tyburn on 1 July 1681, the last Catholic to be martyred there. His relics are enshrined in Downside Abbey; the head is preserved in St Peter's Church, Drogheda. He was beatified in 1920 and canonised on 12 October 1975, the first Irishman to be made a saint since St Laurence O'Toole more than seven hundred years before. Pope John Paul II, as Archbishop of Cracow, led Polish pilgrims at the canonisation.

Drogheda
    Attendance: 300,000
    Concelebrants: 22
    Communion priests: 400
    Communicants: 150,000
    Choir: 1,500
    Stewards: 1,500
    Gardaí: 1,100
    Medical personnel: 50 doctors, 100 nurses, 500 first-aid
          personnel, 1,000 visiting nurses, 36 ambulances
    Deaths: 2
    Births: 0

"There is no such thing as an ordinary layman."

*"Faith and fidelity
are the marks of the
Church in Ireland."*

Address at Drogheda

 Dear brothers and sisters in Jesus Christ.
1. Having greeted the soil of Ireland today on my arrival in Dublin, I make my first Irish journey to this place, to Drogheda. The cry of centuries sends me here.

I arrive as a pilgrim of faith. I arrive also as successor of Peter, to whom Christ has given a particular care for the universal Church. I desire to visit those places in Ireland in particular where the power of God and the action of the Holy Spirit have been specially manifested. I seek first those places which carry in themselves the sign of the "beginning"; and "beginning" is connected with "firstness", with primacy. Such a place on Irish soil is Armagh, for centuries the Episcopal See of the Primate of Ireland.

The Primate is he who has the first place among the bishops, shepherds of the people of God in this land. This primacy is linked to the "beginning" of the faith and of the Church in this country. That is to say, it is linked to the heritage of Saint Patrick, patron of Ireland.

Hence I desired to make my first Irish journey a journey towards the "beginning", the place of the primacy. The Church is built in her entirety on the foundation of the apostles and prophets, Christ Jesus himself being the chief cornerstone (cf Eph 2:20). But in each land and nation the Church has her own particular foundation stone. So it is towards this foundation here in the Primatial See of Armagh that I first direct my pilgrim steps. The See of Armagh is the Primatial See because it is the See of Saint Patrick. The Archbishop of Armagh is Primate of All Ireland today because he is the *Comharba Phádraig,* the successor of Saint Patrick, the first Bishop of Armagh.

2. Standing for the first time on Irish soil, on Armagh soil, the successor of Peter cannot but recall the first coming here, more than one thousand five hundred years ago, of Saint Patrick. From his days as a shepherd boy at Slemish right up to his death at Saul, Patrick was a witness to Jesus Christ. Not far from this spot, on the Hill of Slane, it is said that he lit, for the first time in Ireland, the paschal fire so that the light of Christ might shine forth on all of Ireland and unite all of its people in the love of the one Jesus Christ. It gives me great joy to stand here with you today, within sight of Slane, and to proclaim this same Jesus, the Incarnate Word of God, the Saviour of the world. He is the Lord of history, the Light of the world, the Hope of the future of all humanity. In the words of the Easter liturgy, celebrated for the first time in Ireland by Saint Patrick on the Hill of Slane, we greet Christ today: he is the Alpha and the Omega, the beginning of all things and their end. All time is his and all the ages. To him be glory for ever and ever. Lumen Christi: Deo Gratias. The Light of Christ: Thanks be to God. May the light of Christ, the light of faith continue always to shine out from Ireland. May no darkness ever be able to extinguish it.

That he might be faithful to the end of his life to the light of Christ was Saint

Patrick's prayer for himself. That the people of Ireland might remain faithful always to the light of Christ was his constant prayer for the Irish. He wrote in his *Confession:*

> May God never permit it to happen to me that I should lose his people that he purchased in the utmost parts of the world. I pray to God to give me perseverance and to deign that I be a faithful witness to him to the end of my life for God . . . From the time I came to know him in my youth, the love of God and the fear of him have grown in me, and up to now, thanks to the grace of God, I have kept the faith (*Confession*, 44, 58).

3.   "I have kept the faith." That has been the ambition of the Irish down the centuries. Through persecution and through poverty, in famine and in exile, you have kept the faith. For many it has meant martyrdom. Here at Drogheda, where his relics are honoured, I wish to mention one Irish martyr, Saint Oliver Plunkett, at whose canonisation in the Holy Year, 1975, I was happy to assist, as Cardinal of Cracow, on the invitation of my friend, the late Cardinal Conway. Saint Oliver Plunkett, Primate of Ireland for twelve years, is for ever an outstanding example of the love of Christ for all men. As bishop he preached a message of pardon and peace. He was indeed the defender of the oppressed and the advocate of justice, but he would never condone violence. For men of violence, his word was the word of the Apostle Peter: "Never pay back one wrong with another" (1 Pet 3:9). As a martyr for the faith, he sealed by his death the same message of reconciliation that he had preached during his life. In his heart there was no rancour, for his strength was the love of Jesus, the love of the Good Shepherd who gives his life for his flock. His dying words were words of forgiveness for all his enemies.

4.   Faith and fidelity are the marks of the Church in Ireland, a Church of martyrs, a Church of witnesses; a Church of heroic faith, heroic fidelity. These are the historical signs marking the track of faith on Irish soil. The Gospel and the Church have struck deep roots in the soul of the Irish people. The See of Armagh, the See of Patrick, is the place to see that track, to feel these roots. It is the place in which to meet, from which to address those other great and faithful dioceses whose people have suffered so much from the events of the past decade, Down and Connor, Derry, Dromore, Clogher, Kilmore.

During the period of preparation for my visit to Ireland, especially precious to me was the invitation of the Primate of All Ireland that I should visit his cathedral in Armagh. Particularly eloquent also was the fact that the invitation of the Primate was taken up and repeated by the representatives of the Church of Ireland and by leaders and members of the other Churches, including many from Northern Ireland. For all these invitations I am particularly grateful.

These invitations are an indication of the fact that the Second Vatican Council is achieving its work and that we are meeting with our fellow-Christians of other Churches as people who together confess Jesus Christ as Lord, and who are drawing closer to one another in him as we search for unity and common witness.

This truly fraternal and ecumenical act on the part of representatives of the Churches is also a testimony that the tragic events taking place in Northern Ireland do not have their source in the fact of belonging to different Churches and Confessions; that this is not — despite what is so often repeated before world opinion — a religious war, a struggle between Catholics and Protestants. On the contrary, Catholics and Protestants, as people who confess Christ, taking inspiration from their faith and the Gospel, are seeking to draw closer to one another in unity and peace. When they recall the greatest commandment of Christ, the commandment of love, they cannot behave otherwise.

5. *But Christianity does not command us to close our eyes to difficult human problems.* It does not permit us to neglect and refuse to see unjust social or international situations. What Christianity does forbid is to seek solutions to these situations by the ways of hatred, by the murdering of defenceless people, by the methods of terrorism. Let me say more: Christianity understands and recognises the noble and just struggle for justice; but Christianity is decisively opposed to fomenting hatred and to promoting or provoking violence or struggle for the sake of "struggle". The command, "Thou shalt not kill", must be binding on the conscience of humanity, if the terrible tragedy and destiny of Cain is not to be repeated.

6. For this reason it was fitting for me to come here before going to America, where I hope to address the United Nations Organisation on these same problems of peace and war, justice and human rights. We have decided together, the Cardinal Primate and I, that it would be better for me — for us — to come here, to Drogheda, and that it should be from here that I would render homage to the "beginning" of the faith and to the primacy in your homeland; and from here that I should reflect with all of you, before God, before your splendid Christian history, on this most urgent problem, *the problem of peace and reconciliation.*

We must, above all, clearly realise where the causes of this dramatic struggle are found. We must call by name those systems and ideologies that are responsible for this struggle. We must also reflect whether the ideology of revolution is for the true good of your people, for the true good of man, of mankind. Is it possible to construct the good of individuals and peoples on hatred, on war? Is it right to push the young generations into the pit of fratricide? Is it not necessary to seek solutions to our problems by a different way? Does not the fratricidal struggle make it even more urgent for us to seek peaceful solutions with all our energies? These questions I shall be discussing before the United Nations Assembly in a few days. Here today, in this beloved land of Ireland, from which so many before me have departed for America, I wish to discuss them with you.

7. My message to you today cannot be different from what Saint Patrick and Saint Oliver Plunkett taught you. I preach what they preach: Christ, who is the "Prince of Peace" (Is 9:5); who reconciled us to God and to each other (cf 2 Cor 5:18); who is the source of all unity.

The Gospel reading tells us of Jesus as "the Good Shepherd", whose one desire is to bring all together into one flock. I come to you in his name, in the name of Jesus Christ, who died in order "to come into one the children of God who are scattered abroad" (Jn 11:52). This is my mission, my message to you: Jesus Christ who is our peace. Christ "is our peace" (Eph 2:11). And today and for ever he repeats to us: "My peace I give to you, my peace I leave with you" (Jn 14:27). Never before in the history of mankind has peace been so much talked about and so ardently desired as in our day. The growing interdependence of peoples and nations makes almost everyone subscribe — at least in principle — to the ideal of universal human brotherhood. Great international institutions debate humanity's peaceful coexistence. Public opinion is growing in consciousness of the absurdity of war as a means to resolve differences. More and more, peace is seen as a necessary condition for fraternal relations among nations, and among peoples. Peace is more and more clearly seen as the only way to justice; peace is itself the work of justice. And yet, again and again, one can see how peace is undermined and destroyed. Why is it then that our convictions do not always match our behaviour and our attitudes? Why is it that we do not seem to be able to banish all conflicts from our lives?

8. Peace is the result of many converging attitudes and realities; it is the product of moral concerns of ethical principles based on the Gospel message and fortified by it.

I want to mention here in the first place: justice. In his message for the 1971 Day of Peace, my revered predecessor, that pilgrim for peace, Paul VI, said:

> True peace must be founded upon justice, upon a sense of the untouchable dignity of man, upon the recognition of an indelible and happy equality between men, upon the basic principle of human brotherhood, that is, of the respect and love due to each man, because he is man.

This same message I affirmed in Mexico and in Poland. I reaffirm it here in Ireland. Every human being has inalienable rights that must be respected. Each human community — ethnic, historical, cultural or religious — has rights which must be respected. Peace is threatened every time one of these is violated. The moral law, guardian of human rights, protector of the dignity of man, cannot be set aside by any person or group, or by the State itself, for any cause, not even for security or in the interests of law and order. The law of God stands in judgement over all reasons of State. As long as injustices exist in any of the areas that touch upon the dignity of the human person, be it in the political, social or economic field, be it in the cultural or religious sphere, true peace will not exist. The causes of inequalities must be identified through a courageous and objective evaluation, and they must be eliminated so that every person can develop and grow in the full measure of his or her humanity.

9.   Secondly, peace cannot be established by violence, peace can never flourish in a climate of terror, intimidation and death. It is Jesus himself who said: "All who take the sword will perish by the sword" (Mt 26:52). This is the word of God, and it commands this generation of violent men to desist from hatred and violence and to repent.

I join my voice today to the voice of Paul VI and my other predecessors, to the voices of your religious leaders, to the voices of all men and women of reason, and I proclaim, with the conviction of my faith in Christ and with an awareness of my mission, that violence is evil, that violence is unacceptable as a solution to problems, that violence is unworthy of man. Violence is a lie, for it goes against the truth of our faith, the truth of our humanity. Violence destroys what it claims to defend: the dignity, the life, the freedom of human beings. Violence is a crime against humanity, for it destroys the very fabric of society. I pray with you that the moral sense and Christian conviction of Irish men and women may never become obscured and blunted by the lie of violence, that nobody may ever call murder by any other name than murder, that the spiral of violence may never be given the distinction of unavoidable logic or necessary retaliation. Let us remember that the word remains for ever: "All who take the sword will perish by the sword."

10.   There is another word that must be part of the vocabulary of every Christian, especially when barriers of hate and mistrust have been constructed. This word is *reconciliation*. "So if you are offering your gift at the altar, and there remember that your brother has something against you, leave your gift there before the altar and go; be reconciled with your brother, and then come and offer your gift" (Mt 5:23-24). This command of Jesus is stronger than any barrier that human inadequacy or malice can build. Even when our belief in the fundamental goodness of every human being has been shaken or undermined, even if long-held convictions and attitudes have hardened our hearts, there is one source of power that is stronger than every disappointment, bitterness or ingrained mistrust, and that power is Jesus Christ, who brought forgiveness and reconciliation to the world.

I appeal to all who listen to me; to all who are discouraged after the many years of strife, violence and alienation — that they attempt the seemingly impossible to put an end to the intolerable. I pay homage to the many efforts that have been made by countless men and women in Northern Ireland to walk the path of reconciliation and peace. The courage, the patience, the indomitable hope of the men and women of peace have lighted up the darkness of these years of trial. The spirit of Christian forgiveness shown by so many who have suffered in their persons or through their loved ones has given inspiration to multitudes. In the years to come, when the words of hatred and the deeds of violence are forgotten, it is the words of love and the acts of peace and forgiveness which will be remembered. It is these which will inspire the generations to come.

To all of you who are listening I say: do not believe in violence; do not support violence. It is not the Christian way. It is not the way of the Catholic Church. Believe in peace and forgiveness and love; for they are of Christ.

Communities who stand together in their acceptance of Jesus' supreme message of love, expressed in peace and reconciliation, and in their rejection of all violence, constitute an irresistible force for achieving what many have come to accept as impossible and destined to remain so.

11.   Now I wish to speak to all men and women engaged in violence. I appeal to you, in language of passionate pleading. On my knees I beg you to turn away from the paths of violence and to return to the ways of peace. You may claim to seek justice. I, too, believe in justice and seek justice. But violence only delays the day of justice. Violence destroys the work of justice. Further violence in Ireland will only drag down to ruin the land you claim to love and the values you claim to cherish. In the name of God I beg you: return to Christ, who died so that men might live in forgiveness and peace. He is waiting for you, longing for each one of you to come to him so that he may say to each of you: your sins are forgiven; go in peace.

"The young are the strength of the Pope."

12.   I appeal to young people who may have become caught up in organisations engaged in violence. I say to you, with all the love I have for you, with all the trust I have in young people: do not listen to voices which speak the language of hatred, revenge, retaliation. Do not follow any leaders who train you in the ways of inflicting death. Love live, respect life; in yourselves and in others. Give yourselves to the service of life, not the work of death. Do not think that courage and strength are proved by killing and destruction. The true courage lies in working for peace. The true strength lies in joining with the young men and women of your generation everywhere in building up a just and human and Christian society by the ways of peace. Violence is the enemy of justice. Only peace can lead the way to true justice.

My dear young people; if you have been caught up in the ways of violence, even if you have done deeds of violence, come back to Christ, whose parting gift to the world was peace. Only when you come back to Christ will you find peace for your troubled consciences, and rest for your disturbed souls.

And to you fathers and mothers I say: teach your children how to forgive, make your homes places of love and forgiveness; make your streets and neighbourhoods centres of peace and reconciliation. It would be a crime against youth and their future to let even one child grow up with nothing but the experience of violence and hate.

13.   Now I wish to speak to all the people in positions of leadership, to all who can influence public opinion, to all members of political parties and to all who support them. I say to you:

Never think you are betraying your own community by seeking to understand and respect and accept those of a different tradition. You will serve your own tradition best by working for reconciliation with the others. Each of the historical communities in Ireland can only harm itself by seeking to harm the other. Continued violence can only endanger everything that is most precious in the traditions and aspirations of both communities.

Let no one concerned with Ireland have any illusions about the nature and the menace of political violence. The ideology and the methods of violence have become an international problem of the utmost gravity. The longer the violence continues in Ireland, the more the danger will grow that this beloved land could become yet another theatre for international terrorism.

14.   To all who bear political responsibility for the affairs of Ireland, I want to speak with the same urgency and intensity with which I have spoken to the men of violence. Do not cause or condone or tolerate conditions which give excuse or pretext to men of violence. Those who resort to violence always claim that only violence brings about change. They claim that political action cannot achieve justice. You politicians must prove them to be wrong. You must show that there is a peaceful, political way to justice. You must show that peace achieves the works of justice, and violence does not.

I urge you who are called to the noble vocation of politics to have the courage to face up to your responsibility, to be leaders in the cause of peace, reconciliation and justice. If politicians do not decide and act for just change, then the field is left open to the men of violence. Violence thrives best when there is a political vacuum and a refusal of political movement. Paul VI, writing to Cardinal Conway in March 1972, said:

> Everyone must play his part. Obstacles which stand in the way of justice must be removed: obstacles such as civil inequity, social and political discrimination, and misunderstanding between individuals and groups. There must be a mutual and abiding respect for others: for their persons, their rights and their lawful aspirations.

I make these words of my revered predecessor my own today.

15.   I came to Drogheda today on a great mission of peace and reconciliation. I come as a pilgrim of peace, Christ's peace. To Catholics, to Protestants, my message is peace and love. May no Irish Protestant think that the Pope is an enemy, a danger or a threat. My desire is that, instead, Protestants would see in me a friend and a brother in Christ. Do not lose trust that this visit of mine may be fruitful, that this voice of mine may be listened to. And even if it were not listened to, let history record that at a difficult moment in the experience of the people of Ireland, the Bishop of Rome set foot in your land, that he was with you and prayed with you for peace and reconciliation, for the victory of justice and love over hatred and violence. Yes, this our witness finally becomes a prayer, a prayer from the heart for peace for the peoples who live on this earth, peace for all the people of Ireland.

Let this fervent prayer for peace penetrate with light all consciences. Let it purify them and take hold of them.

Christ, Prince of Peace;
Mary, Mother of Peace, Queen of Ireland;
Saint Patrick, Saint Oliver, and all saints of Ireland;
I, together with all those gathered here and with all who join with me, invoke you,
Watch over Ireland. Protect humanity. Amen.

"*It is not what you do that matters most: but what you are.*"

Clonmacnois

Clonmacnois was founded around 545 by St Ciarán, a Connacht man with a magnetic personality, who died — like Christ — at the age of thirty-three. Like Christ, too, St Ciarán attracted an untold number of disciples, and his foundation was soon held in the greatest of respect by king and cleric alike.

Situated at a crossroads where an important east-west artery bridged the north-south flowing Shannon, Clonmacnois was a cosmopolitan meeting place. Despite the fact that its accessibility also made it a prey for Viking, Norman and Irish plunderers, its own internal strength enabled it to survive for more than a thousand years, and to this day its name is still enshrined in the title of the diocese in which it lies.

The green open spaces where the noble stone monuments now proudly stand were once the site of a multitude of wooden huts which housed not only monks, but innumerable students from far and near. For Clonmacnois had a strong literary tradition, and the annals which its monks kept are an important source for the early history of Ireland.

Clonmacnois occupies a prominent place in the history of Irish art and architecture — a fact emphasised by the Holy Father in the address which he gave there. On the altar during the Pope's visit were two pieces of metalwork which may have emanated from the metal workshops for which Clonmacnois was famous — the Crozier of St Mel (ninth or tenth century) and the marvellously decorated twelfth-century Shrine of St Manchan, brought respectively from Longford and from Boher parish church for the occasion.

Clonmacnois can be proud of the greatest known collection of early Irish gravestones, laid flat over the burial-places of pious monks who died there between the eighth and the twelfth centuries. It can boast, also, of two round towers. One is free-standing; the other acted as belfry for St Finghin's church down near the water's edge. In addition to the cathedral which forms the centrepiece of the ancient monastry, Clonmacnois has a number of smaller churches. These include the miniature structure venerated as the burial place of St Ciarán, and the hauntingly beautiful Romanesque church placed outside the sacred enclosure for the nuns who were once attached to the monastery.

But pride of place among all the stone monuments at Clonmacnois must go to the high crosses — an art form in the development of which Clonmacnois probably played a very significant rôle. The greatest of these is the early ninth-century Cross of the Scriptures, the west face of which tells the story of the passion and death of Our Lord, while the centre of the east face is occupied by the Last Judgement. Immediately below this latter, Pope John Paul II came face to face both with a namesake and with his first predecessor. For, on the cross is a panel showing Christ in the centre presenting a book to St Paul on the right and a key to St Peter on the left. Little did its carver think that more than a thousand years later a Pope would come to admire his workmanship!

Clonmacnois
  Attendance: 20,000
  Stewards: 150
  Medical and other personnel: 2 doctors, 4 nurses, 2
        ambulances, 14 fire officers, 4 fire tenders
  Gifts given to the Pope: *Cluan Chiaráin* by Rev. John
        Corkery; *Short History of Clonmacnois, the
        Shrine of St Manchan and Crozier of St Mel*,
        one volume bound in oak, from Roscrea
        Monastery; an album of photographs of
        Clonmacnois, from Midland Regional Tourism
        and Bord Fáilte; *Peace — The Work of Justice*
        by Bishop Cahal B. Daly

"Throughout the ages."

"When we look at the works of faith, we must give thanks to God."

Address at Clonmacnois

Dear brothers and sisters,
This visit to Clonmacnois gives me the opportunity to render homage to the traditions of faith and Christian living in Ireland.

In particular, I wish to recall and honour the great monastic contribution to Ireland that was made here on this revered spot for one thousand years, and whose influence was carried all over Europe by missionary monks and by students of this monastic school of Clonmacnois.

When we look at the works of faith, we must give thanks to God. Thanks to God for the origins of this apostolic faith in Ireland. Thanks to God for the saints and apostles and all who were the instruments for implanting and keeping alive this faith, and who "have done God's will throughout the ages". Thanks to God for the generosity of faith that brought forth fruits of justice and holiness of life. Thanks to God for the preservation of the faith in integrity and purity of teaching. Thanks to God for the continuity of the message of the apostles handed down intact to this day.

Never forget the wonderful boast and commitment made by Saint Columban to Bóniface IV in Rome: "We Irish . . . are disciples of Saints Peter and Paul . . .; we hold unbroken that Catholic faith which we first received from you."

And in Ireland today this Catholic faith is unbroken, alive and active by the merits of Our Lord Jesus Christ; and by the power of his grace we can and must always be this way in Ireland.

Clonmacnois was long the centre of a renowned school of sacred art. The Shrine of Saint Manchan, standing on the altar today, is one outstanding example of its work. This is therefore a fitting place for me to express my gratitude for the works of Irish sacred art, several pieces of which have been presented to me on the occasion of my visit.

Irish art embodies in many instances the deep faith and devotion of the Irish people as expressed in the personal sensitivity of its artists. Every piece of art, be it religious or secular, be it a painting, a sculpture, a poem or any form of handicraft made with loving skill, is a sign and a symbol of the inscrutable secret of human existence, of man's origin and destiny, of the meaning of his life and work. It speaks to us of the meaning of birth and death, of the greatness of man.

Praised be Jesus Christ!

"I wish to recall and honour the great monastic contribution to Ireland that was made here on this revered spot for one thousand years . . ."

Galway

Galway, the principal city of the province of Connacht as well as the county of Galway, has a seaport, industries, a university college and, since 1965, a new cathedral. Its population is 37,000. At the gateway to Connemara is Salthill, a suburb of the city, one of the best-known tourist centres in the country.

The diocese of Galway, dating only from 1831, is the youngest in the country. Two smaller dioceses, Kilmacduagh and Kilfenora, were subsequently added to it. Galway town was a Norman settlement of some importance. The citizens carefully avoided any assimilation with the surrounding native Irish. Thus there were inevitable conflicts — in the ecclesiastical as well as other spheres. The Norman settlers did not wish to be ruled by Irish clergy, and petitioned the Pope to grant them exemption from Irish clerical rule. Thus, in 1484 Pope Innocent VII granted in the Bull, *Super Gregem Dominicum,* that henceforth the mayor and burgesses would elect a "warden" and eight parish priests at regular intervals. The warden, a priest, was head of the Church in Galway, and had quasi-episcopal functions. Thus, from 1464 till 1831, the Church in Galway had a form of limited democracy not known elsewhere.

Gradually, prominent Galway families (called tribes) gained control of the wardenship and refused to extend electoral power more widely, even at the request of the Holy See. Finally, after some wrangling, the tribes gave in and the diocese of Galway was founded and given its own bishop.

It was a small and poor diocese, even after the inclusion of Kilmacduagh and Kilfenora. Consequently, it was not possible to undertake construction of a cathedral until 1957. Under the direction of Bishop Michael Browne the great work was completed in 1965, when it was dedicated to Our Lady Assumed into Heaven and St Nicholas.

Eyre Square, statue of Pádraig Ó Conaire

Ballybrit

The racecourse at Ballybrit is where the annual well-known and very colourful Galway races take place. For over 150 years it has been the great summer outing for very many people. The chairman of the race committee, Lord Killanin, who is also chairman of the International Olympic Committee, together with Bishop Casey of Galway, received the Pope at Ballybrit.

A few feet from the base of the papal altar is, appropriately enough, an old Mass rock used in penal times, when saying Mass in town was a risk.

Galway
    Attendance: 300,000 (200,000 young people)
    Concelebrants: 85
    Communion priests: 800
    Communicants: 150,000
    Choirs: 2 — 100 in each
    Stewards: 2,400
    Deaths: 1
    Births: 2
    Gifts offered: 26 oak saplings (one for each diocese); the
            Offertory procession depicted various aspects
            of life and occupations — national teacher,
            nurse, married couple with baby, soldier, novice
            postulant (female), novice brother, religious,
            the blind, athlete, the lame, garda, carpenter,
            mechanic, baker, musician, farmer, fisherman,
            student, waitress, air hostess, dancer, itinerant,
            secretary, the deaf, naval cadet, "Mr everybody"

Address on arrival at Galway

I thank the Bishop of Galway and Kilmacduagh and the esteemed Mayor of the City of Galway for this warm welcome. It is a special pleasure for me to be able to come west today across the width of Ireland to beautiful Galway Bay. To you, dear brother, pastor of this western see which in Saint Patrick's time was "beyond the confines of the inhabited earth", but which now is at the meeting place of Europe and the Americas — to you and to your priests, religious and laity I extend a word of special greeting. It honours your diocese and your city that you invited me to meet with representatives of all the youth of Ireland. Among you I shall meet the future of Ireland, those who will carry the torch of the Christian faith into the twenty-first century.

On this first visit of the Vicar of Christ on earth to the people of the West of Ireland, I wish to ask your prayerful support for my universal mission as Bishop of Rome. I count in a special way on your daily prayers for me in your families, when parents and children together invoke the help of the Lord Jesus and of his Mother Mary.

May God bless this city and all its inhabitants, and grant his strength to the weak and the sick, his courage to those who struggle, and his peace and joy to all.

Homily at the Mass for the Youth of Ireland, Galway

A aos óg na hÉireann, go mbeannaí Dia dhibh!

Dear young people, brothers and sisters of Our Lord Jesus Christ,

1.   This is a very special occasion, a very important one. This morning, the Pope belongs to the youth of Ireland! I have looked forward to this moment; I have prayed that I may touch your hearts with the words of Jesus. Here I wish to recall what I said so often before as Archbishop of Cracow and what I have repeated as successor of Saint Peter: I believe in youth. I believe in youth with all my heart and with all the strength of my conviction. And to day I say: I believe in the youth of Ireland! I believe in you who stand before me, in every one of you.

When I look at you, I see the Ireland of the future. Tomorrow, you will be the living force of your country; you will decide what Ireland will be. Tomorrow, as technicians or teachers, nurses or secretaries, farmers or tradesmen, doctors or engineers, priests or religious — tomorrow you will have the power to make dreams come true. Tomorrow, Ireland will depend on you.

When I look at you assembled around this altar and listen to your praying voices, your singing voices, I see the future of the Church. God has his plan for the Church in Ireland, but he needs you to carry it out. What the Church will be in the future depends on your free cooperation with God's grace.

When I look at the thousands of young people here before me, I also see the challenges that you face. You have come from the parishes of Ireland as the representatives of those that could not be here. You carry in your hearts the rich heritage that you have received from your parents, your teachers and your priests. You carry in your hearts the treasures which Irish history and culture have given you, but you also share in the problems that Ireland faces.

"The Eucharist is a challenge to our daily lives."

2.   Today, for the first time since Saint Patrick preached the faith to the Irish, the successor of Peter comes from Rome and sets foot on Irish soil. You rightly ask yourselves what message he brings and what words he will speak to Ireland's youth. My message can be none other than the message of Christ himself; my words can be none other than the word of God.

I did not come here to give you an answer to all your individual questions. You have your bishops, who know your local circumstances and local problems; you have your priests, especially those who devote themselves to the demanding but rewarding pastoral care of youth. They know you personally and will help you to find the right answers. But, I too feel that I know you, for I know and understand young people. And I know that you, like other young people of your age in other countries, are affected by what is happening in society around you. Although you still live in an atmosphere where true religious and moral principles are held in honour, you have to realise that your fidelity to these principles will be tested in many ways. The religious and moral traditions of Ireland, the very soul of Ireland, will be challenged by temptations that spare no society in our age. Like so many other young people in various parts of the world, you will be told that changes must be made, that you must have more freedom, that you should be different from your parents, and that the decisions about your lives depend on you, and you alone.

The prospect of growing economic progress, and the chance of obtaining a greater share of the goods that modern society has to offer, will appear to you as an opportunity to achieve greater freedom. The more you possess — you may be tempted to think — the more you will feel liberated from every type of confinement. In order to

"The Eucharist is a promise of eternal life."

make more money and to possess more, in order to eliminate effort and worry, you may be tempted to take moral shortcuts where honesty, truth and work are concerned. The progress of science and technology seems inevitable and you may be enticed to look towards the technological society for the answers to all your problems.

3.   The lure of pleasure, to be had whenever and wherever it can be found, will be strong and it may be presented to you as part of progress towards greater autonomy and freedom from rules. The desire to be free from external restraints may manifest itself very strongly in the sexual domain, since this is an area that it so closely tied to a human personality. The moral standards that the Church and society have held up to you for so long a time will be presented as obsolete and a hindrance to the full development of your own personality. Mass media, entertainment, and literature will present a model for living where all too often it is every man for himself, and where the unrestrained affirmation of self leaves no room for concern for others.

You will hear people tell you that your religious practices are hopelessly out of date, that they hamper your style and your future, that with everything that social and scientific progress has to offer, you will be able to organise your own lives, and that God has played out his rôle. Even many religious persons will adopt such attitudes, breathing them in from the surrounding atmosphere, without attending to the practical atheism that is at their origin.

A society that, in this way, has lost its higher religious and moral principles will become an easy prey for manipulation and for domination by the forces, which, under the pretext of greater freedom, will enslave it even more.

Yes, dear young people, do not close your eyes to the moral sickness that stalks your society today, and from which your youth alone will not protect you. How many young people have already warped their consciences and have substituted the true joy of life with drugs, sex, alcohol, vandalism and the empty pursuit of mere material possessions.

4.   Something else is needed: something that you will find only in Christ, for he alone is the measure and the scale that you must use to evaluate your own life. In Christ you will discover the true greatness of your own humanity; he will make you understand your own dignity as human beings "created to the image and likeness of God" (Gen 1:26). Christ has the answers to your questions and the key to history; he has the power to uplift hearts. He keeps calling you, he keeps inviting you, he who is "the way, and the truth, and the life" (Jn 14:6). Yes, Christ calls you, but he calls you in truth. His call is demanding, because he invites you to let yourselves be "captured" by him completely, so that your whole lives will be seen in a different light. He is the Son of God, who reveals to you the loving face of the Father. He is the teacher, the only one whose

"Tomorrow, you will have the power to make dreams come true."

teaching does not pass away, the only one who teaches with authority. He is the friend who said to his disciples, "No longer do I call you servants . . . but I have called you friends" (Jn 15:15). And he proved his friendship by laying down his life for you.

His call is demanding for he taught us what it means to be truly human. Without heeding the call of Jesus, it will not be possible to realise the fullness of your own humanity. You must build on the foundation which is Christ (cf 1 Cor 3:11); only with him will your life be meaningful and worthwhile.

You come from Catholic families; you go regularly and meet Christ in Holy Communion on Sundays or even during the week. Many of you pray with your families every day; and I hope you all will continue to do so throughout later life. And yet it can happen that you will be tempted to walk away from Christ. This can happen especially if you see the contradiction in the life of some of your fellow men between the faith they profess and their way of living. But I wish to insist and to plead that you always heed the call of Christ, for he alone can teach you the true meaning of life and of all temporal realities.

"I too feel I know you."

5.   Permit me, in this context, to recall still another phrase of the Gospel, a phrase that we must remember even when its consequences are particularly difficult for us to accept. It is the phrase that Christ pronounced in the Sermon on the Mount: "Love your enemies, do good to those who hate you" (Lk 6:27). You have guessed already that even by my reference to these words of the Saviour, I have before my mind the painful events that for over ten years have been taking place in Northern Ireland. I am sure that all young people are living these events very deeply and very painfully, for they are tracing deep furrows in your young hearts. These events, painful as they are, must also be an incitement to reflection. They demand that you form an interior judgement of conscience to determine where you, as young Catholics, stand on the matter.

You heard the words of Jesus: "Love your enemies." The command of Jesus does not mean that we are not bound by love for our native land; it does not mean that we can remain indifferent before injustice in its various temporal and historical aspects. These words of Jesus take away only hate. I beg you to reflect deeply: what would human life be if Jesus had never spoken such words? What would the world be if in our mutual relations we were to give primacy to hatred among people, between classes, between nations? What would the future of humanity be if we were to base on this hatred the future of individuals and of nations?

"Young people of Ireland, I love you!"

"I believe in youth."

Sometimes, one could have the feeling that, before the experiences of history and before concrete situations, love has lost its power and that it is impossible to practise it. And yet, in the long run, love always brings victory, love is never defeated. And I could add that the history of Ireland proves that, if it were not so, humanity would only be condemned to destruction.

6.   Dear young friends, this is the message I entrust to you today, asking you to take it with you and share it with your family at home and with your friends in school and at work. On returning home, tell your parents, and everyone who wants to listen, that the Pope believes in you and that he counts on you. Say that the young are the strength of the Pope, of the Church, of Ireland, of the world, and that the Pope wishes to share with them his hope for the future, and his encouragement.

I have given you the words of my heart. Now let me also ask you for something in return. You know that from Ireland I am going to the United Nations. The truth which I have proclaimed before you is the same that I shall present, in a different way, before that supreme forum of the nations. I hope that your prayers — the prayers of the youth of Ireland — will accompany me and support me in this important mission. I count on you, because the future of human life on this earth is at stake, in every country and in the whole world. The future of all peoples and nations, the future of humanity itself depends on this: whether the words of Jesus in the Sermon on the Mount, whether the message of the Gospel will be listened to once again.

May the Lord Jesus be always with you! With his truth that makes you free (cf Jn 8:32); with his word that unlocks the mystery of man and reveals to man his own humanity; with his death and resurrection that makes you new and strong.

Let us place this intention at the feet of Mary, Mother of God and Queen of Ireland, example of generous love and dedication to the service of others.

Young people of Ireland, I love you!
Young people of Ireland, I bless you!
I bless you in the name of Our Lord Jesus Christ.
Críost liom, Críost romham, Críost i mo dhiaidh!

Since 1879, the little village of Knock, Co. Mayo, has been attracting pilgrims from Ireland and many other countries to the Shrine of Our Lady. A new church-shelter, built to protect pilgrims, especially the sick, from bad weather, is dedicated to Our Lady Queen of Ireland.

1879 was a year of misery and famine in most of rural Ireland. Many commentators have interpreted the apparition of 21 August of that year as a message of comfort and encouragement to an oppressed people.

The apparition

The apparition first appeared on the southern gable of the church of St John the Baptist, at about seven o'clock on a Thursday evening. It was raining heavily at the time but was still broad daylight. Several passers-by saw what they took to be three statues in front of the gable, or simply "something bright", but they did not pause to investigate the matter further, probably because of the bad weather conditions then prevailing.

It was around eight o'clock before a crowd began to gather. Three life-size figures were then seen to the west of the gable, surrounded by light and standing out in front of it. The one in the middle, somewhat larger than the other two, was immediately identifiable as Our Lady, her eyes lifted to heaven and her hands raised to the shoulders with palms inwards. She was dressed in a full loose cloak and had a beautiful crown on her head. To her right was St Joseph, his head bowed respectfully towards her.

On her left was a figure like a bishop, wearing a small mitre, with the right hand raised as if preaching, and a book of Gospels or Mass book in the left hand. This figure was identified by Mary Byrne, one of the witnesses, as St John the Evangelist because it bore some resemblance to a statue of that saint which she said she had seen in the seaside resort of Lecanvey, near Westport. This statue, a carved wooden one, disappeared when the old church of Lecanvey was replaced by the present one in 1891. The figures did not speak but moved inward toward the gable and outward from it according as the witnesses approached them closer and moved away again.

When night fell, the gable was covered with a cloud of pleasing light, soft like moonlight rather than harsh or glaring. The figures seemed themselves to be made of light, each giving out different degrees of brilliance. The vision lasted for two hours and was seen by, at the very least, twenty-two people. More probably, almost the entire village of Knock saw the apparition.

To the left of St John was an altar on which stood a cross and a lamb. Around the lamb, some of the witnesses saw angels' wings or moving lights. Although it rained all the time, no rain fell on the figures or on the wall behind them, though the wind, from the south, should have driven the rain in that direction. The meadow underneath (examined minutely by one elderly witness) remained bone-dry. This reversal of the usual order of nature is regarded as a miracle, confirming the divine origin of the apparition. Rain flowed on each side of the gable and formed pools of water there. But it remained quite dry where the figures were.

Eventually, all who were still there left the gable together to look after a sick woman, Mrs Campbell, who had collapsed at her doorway in attempting to see the vision. They thought she was on the point of death but she did not die that night. When they returned, the apparition was gone.

Claimed miracles of healing at Knock

Hundreds, possibly thousands, of claimed miracles of healing have occurred at Knock since the apparition of 21 August 1879. Archdeacon Bartholomew Cavanagh, P.P., began keeping a diary of such cures on 31 October 1879. The *Weekly News* started the publication of this diary on 6 March 1880. By 9 October 1880, this list of claimed miracles of healing had reached over 600. Included were letters reporting cures written to both the local newspapers and the priest of Knock.

A second diary of cures at Knock was kept by Mr John A. Gibney of 3 Palmerston Place, Broadstone, Dublin. In January 1880, he himself was cured instantaneously of advanced T.B. of the hip. Solemnly attesting his diary to be true, he lodged it with the Archbishop of Tuam. His account of apparent miracles is similar to Archdeacon Cavanagh's diary in that it seems to contain a mixture of truly miraculous occurrences with other vague accounts of benefits received.

A Medical Bureau was established at Knock in 1936 but it ceased to function there after about ten years. Possibly because of the heavy workload already carried by the local general practitioners, who offered their voluntary services to the Bureau, it was never adequately organised.

Knock
  Attendance: 450,000
  Concelebrants: 200 (156 bishops and cardinals, 44
          priests)
  Communion priests: 1,000
  Communicants: 200,000
  Choir: 160
  Stewards: 6,000
  Gardaí: 500
  Army and FCA: 2,000
  Scouts: 500
  Sick: 2,500
  Medical personel: 50 doctors, 150 nurses, 1,300 other
          medical personnel
  Gifts offered: broken wheel (relating to the story of St
          Jarlath); stone from Croagh Patrick; cross and
          rose (suffering); original Galway rosary, brought
          in by Franciscans in penal times; water from
          the holy well of Lispatrick; plaque representing
          the missionary activity of the Irish Church;
          flowers representing first communicants,
          presented by boy and girl for the Year of the
          Child
  Gifts given to the Pope: Desmond Kyne's kinetic
          engraving of Our Lady Queen of Ireland
  Gift from the Pope: a golden rose

Toward the end of the Mass at Knock the Pope read a
document erecting the Church of Our Lady Queen of
Ireland as the Basilica of Our Lady Queen of Ireland and
presented a golden rose, symbolic of the high status of the
Shrine.

Homily at Knock

Sé do bheatha, a Mhuire, atá lán de ghrásta . . .

Dear brothers and sisters in Christ, faithful sons and daughters of Mary,

1. Here I am at the goal of my journey to Ireland: the Shrine of Our Lady at Knock. Since I first learnt of the centenary of this Shrine, which is being celebrated this year, I have felt a strong desire to come here, the desire to make yet another pilgrimage to the Shrine of the Mother of Christ, the Mother of the Church, the Queen of Peace. Do not be surprised at this desire of mine. It has been my custom to make pilgrimages to the shrines of Our Lady, starting with my earliest youth and in my own country. I made such pilgrimages also as a bishop and as a cardinal. I know very well that every people, every country, indeed every diocese, has its *holy places* in which *the heart of the whole people of God beats, one could say, in more lively fashion*: places of special encounter between God and human beings; places in which Christ dwells in a special way in our midst. If these places are so often dedicated to his Mother, it reveals all the more fully to us the nature of his Church. Since the Second Vatican Council, which concluded its *Constitution on the Church* with the chapter on "The Blessed Virgin Mary, Mother of God, in the Mystery of Christ and of the Church", this fact is more evident for us today than ever — yes, for all of us, for all Christians. Do we not confess with all our brethren, even with those with whom we are not yet linked in full unity, that we are *a pilgrim people.* As once this people travelled on its pilgrimage under the guidance of Moses, so we, the People of God of the New Covenant, are travelling on our pilgrim way under the guidance of Christ.

I am here then as a pilgrim, a sign of the pilgrim Church throughout the world participating, through my presence as Peter's successor, in a very special way in the centenary celebration of this Shrine.

The liturgy of the word of today's Mass gives me my pilgrim's salutation to Mary, as now I come before her in Ireland's Marian Shrine at Cnoc Mhuire, the Hill of Mary.

"We entrust to your motherly care the land of Ireland."

2.   "Blessed are you among women, and blessed is the fruit of your womb" (Lk 1:42). These are the words with which Elizabeth, filled with the Holy Spirit, greeted Mary, her kinswoman from Nazareth.

"Blessed are you among women, and blessed is the fruit of your womb!" This is also my greeting to Muire Máthair Dé, Mary the Mother of God, Queen of Ireland, at this Shrine of Knock. With these words, I want to express the immense joy and gratitude that fills my heart today in this place. I could not have wanted it any differently. Highlights of my recent pastoral journeys have been the visits to the shrines of Mary: to Our Lady of Guadalupe in Mexico, to the Black Madonna of Jasna Góra in my homeland, and three weeks ago to Our Lady of Loreto in Italy. Today I come here because I want all of you to know that my devotion to Mary unites me, in a very special way, with the people of Ireland.

3.   Yours is a long spiritual tradition of devotion of Our Lady. Mary can truly say of Ireland what we have just heard in the first reading: "So I took root in an honoured people" (Sir 24:12). Your veneration of Mary is so deeply interwoven in your faith that its origins are lost in the early centuries of the evangelisation of your country. I have been told that, in Irish speech, the names of God and Jesus and Mary are linked with one another, and that God is seldom named in prayer or in blessing without Mary's name being mentioned also. I also know that you have an eight-century Irish poem that calls Mary "Sun of our race", and that a litany from that same period honours her as "Mother of the heavenly and earthly Church". But better than any literary source, it is the constant and deeply rooted devotion to Mary that testifies to the success of evangelisation by Saint Patrick, who brought you the Catholic faith in all its fullness.

It is fitting then, and it gives me great happiness to see, that the Irish people maintain this traditional devotion to the Mother of God in their homes and their parishes, and in a special way at this Shrine of Cnoc Mhuire. For a whole century now, you have sanctified this place of pilgrimage through your prayers, through your sacrifices, through your penance. All those who have come here have received blessings through the intercession of Mary. From that day of grace, 21 August 1879, until this very day, the sick and suffering, people handicapped in body or mind, troubled in their faith or their conscience, all have been healed, comforted and confirmed in their faith because they trusted that the Mother of God would lead them to her Son, Jesus. Every time a pilgrim comes up to what was once an obscure bogside village in County Mayo, every time a man, woman or child comes up to the old church with the apparition gable or to the new Shrine of Mary Queen of Ireland, it is to renew his or her faith in the salvation that comes through Jesus, who made us all children of God and heirs of the kingdom of heaven. By entrusting yourselves to Mary, you receive Christ. In Mary, "the Word was made flesh"; in her the Son of God became man, so that all of us might know how great our human dignity is. Standing on this hallowed ground, we look up to the Mother of God and say: "Blessed are you among women, and blessed is the fruit of your womb."

The present time is an important moment in the history of the universal Church, and, in particular, of the Church in Ireland. So many things have changed. So many valuable new insights have been gained in what it means to be Christian. So many new problems have to be faced by the faithful, either because of the increased pace of change in society, or because of the new demands that are made on the people of God — demands to live to the fullest the mission of evangelisation. The Second Vatican Council and the Synod of Bishops have brought new pastoral vitality to the whole Church. My revered predecessor, Paul VI, laid down wise guidelines for renewal and

gave the whole people of God inspiration and enthusiasm for the task. In everything he said and did, Paul VI taught the Church to be open to the needs of humanity and at the same time to be unfailingly faithful to the unchanging message of Christ. Loyal to the teaching of the College of Bishops together with the Pope, the Church in Ireland has gratefully accepted the riches of the Council and the Synods. The Irish Catholic people have clung faithfully, sometimes in spite of pressures to the contrary, to the rich expressions of faith, to the fervent sacramental practices, and to that dedication to charity, which have always been a special mark of your Church. But the task of renewal in Christ is never finished. Every generation, with its own mentality and characteristics, is like a new continent to be won for Christ. The Church must constantly look for new ways that will enable her to understand more profoundly and to carry out with renewed vigour the mission received from her founder. In this arduous task, like so many times before when the Church was faced with a new challenge, we turn to Mary, the Mother of God and the Seat of Wisdom, trusting that she will show us again the way to her Son. A very old Irish homily for the feast of the Ephiphany (from the *Leabhar Breac*) says that as the Wise Men found Jesus on the lap of his Mother, so we today find Christ on the lap of the Church.

4. Mary was truly united with Jesus. Not many of her own words have been preserved in the Gospels; but those that have been recorded refer us again to her Son and to his word. At Cana in Galilee, she turned from her Son to the servants and said "Do whatever he tells you" (Jn 2:5). This same message, she still speaks to us today.

5. "Do whatever he tells you." What Jesus tells us — through his life and by his word — has been preserved for us in the Gospels, and in the letters of the apostles and of Saint Paul and transmitted to us by the Church. We must make ourselves familiar with his words. We do this by listening to the readings from sacred scripture in the liturgy of the word, which introduce us to the Eucharistic sacrifice; by reading the scriptures on our own, in the family, or together with friends; by reflecting on what the Lord tells us when we recite the rosary and combine our devotion to the Mother of God with prayerful meditation on the mysteries of her Son's life. Whenever we have questions, whenever we are burdened, whenever we are faced with the choices that our faith imposes on us, the word of the Lord will comfort and guide us.

Christ has not left his followers without guidance in the task of understanding and living the Gospel. Before returning to his Father, he promised to send his Holy Spirit to the Church: "But the Counsellor, the Holy Spirit whom the Father will send in my name, he will teach you all things, and bring to your remembrance all I have said to you" (Jn 14:26).

This same Spirit guides the successors of the apostles, your bishops, united with the Bishop of Rome, to whom it was entrusted to preserve the faith and to "preach the Gospel to the whole creation" (Mk 16:14). Listen to their voices, for they bring you the word of the Lord.

6. "Do whatever he tells you." So many different voices assail the Christian in today's wonderful but complicated and demanding world. So many false voices are heard that conflict with the word of the Lord. They are the voices that tell you that truth is less important than personal gain; that comfort, wealth, and pleasure are the true aims of life; that the refusal of new life is better than generosity of spirit and the taking up of responsibility; that justice must be achieved but without any personal involvement by the Christian; that violence can be a means to a good end; that unity can be built without giving up hate.

And now let us return in thought from Cana in Galilee to the Shrine of Knock. Do we not hear the Mother of Christ pointing him out to us here too, and speaking to us the same words that she used at Cana: "Do whatever he tells you"? She is saying it to all of us. Her voice is heard more expressly by my brothers in the episcopate, the pastors of the Church in Ireland, who by inviting me here have asked me to respond to an invitation from the Mother of the Church. And so, venerable brothers, I am responding, as I enter in thought into the whole of your county's past and as I feel also the force of its eloquent present, so joyful and yet at the same time so anxious and at times so sorrowful. I am responding, as I did at Guadalupe in Mexico and at Jasna Góra in Poland. In my own name and on your behalf and in the name of all the Catholic people of Ireland, I pronounce, at the close of this homily, the following words of trust and consecration:

Mother, in this Shrine you gather the People of God of all Ireland and constantly point out to them Christ in the Eucharist and in the Church. At this solemn moment *we listen* with particular attention to your words: "Do whatever my Son tells you." And *we wish* to respond to your words with all our heart. We wish to do what your Son tells us, what he commands us, for he has the words of eternal life. We wish to carry out and fulfil all that comes from him, all that is contained in the Good News, as our forefathers did for many centuries. Their fidelity to Christ and to his Church, and their heroic attachment to the Apostolic See, have in a way stamped on all of us an indelible mark that we all share. Their fidelity has, over the centuries, borne fruit in Christian heroism and in a virtuous tradition of living in accordance with God's law,

especially in accordance with the holiest commandment of the Gospel — the commandment of love. We have received this splendid heritage from their hands at the beginning of a new age, as we approach the close of the second millennium since the Son of God was born of you, our *alma Mater,* and we intend to *carry this heritage into the future* with the same fidelity with which our forefathers bore witness to it.

Today therefore, on the occasion of the first visit of a Pope to Ireland, we entrust and consecrate to you, Mother of Christ and Mother of the Church, our hearts, our consciences, and our works, in order that they may be in keeping with the faith we profess. We entrust and consecrate to you each and every one of those who make up both the community of the Irish people and the community of the people of God living in this land.

We entrust and consecrate to you the bishops of Ireland, the clergy, the religious men and women, the contemplative monks and sisters, the seminarists, the novices. We entrust and consecrate to you the mothers and fathers, the youth, the children. We entrust and consecrate to you the teachers, the catechists, the students, the writers, the poets, the actors, the artists, the workers and their leaders, the employers and managers, the professional people, the farmers; those engaged in political and public life; those who form public opinion. We entrust and consecrate to you the married and those preparing for marriage; those called to serve you and their fellow. men in single life; the sick, the aged, the mentally ill, the handicapped and all who nurse and care for them. We entrust and consecrate to you the prisoners and all who feel rejected; the exiled, the homesick and the lonely.

We entrust to your motherly care the land of Ireland, where you have been and are so much loved. Help this land to stay true to you and your Son always. May prosperity never cause Irish men and women to forget God or abandon their faith. Keep them faithful in prosperity to the faith they would not surrender in poverty and persecution. Save them from greed, from envy, from seeking selfish or sectional interest. Help them to work together with a sense of Christian purpose and a common Christian goal, to build a just and peaceful and loving society where the poor are never neglected and the rights of all, especially the weak, are respected. Queen of Ireland, Mary Mother of the heavenly and earthly Church, Máthair Dé, keep Ireland true to her spiritual tradition and her Christian heritage. Help her to respond to her historic mission of bringing the light of Christ to the nations, and so making the glory of God be the honour of Ireland.

Mother, can we keep silent about what we find most painful, what leaves us many a time so helpless? In a very special way we entrust to you this great wound now afflicting our people, hoping that your hands will be able to cure and heal it. Great is our concern for those young souls who are caught up in bloody acts of vengeance and hatred. Mother, do not abandon these youthful hearts. Mother, be with them in their most dreadful hours, when we can neither counsel nor assist them. Mother, protect all of us and especially the youth of Ireland from being overcome by hostility and hatred. Teach us to distinguish clearly what proceeds from love for our country from what bears the mark of destruction and the brand of Cain. Teach us that evil means can never lead to a good end; that all human life is sacred; that murder is murder no matter what the motive or end. Save others, those who view these terrible events, from another danger: that of living a life robbed of Christian ideals or in conflict with the principles of morality.

May our ears constantly hear with the proper clarity your motherly voice: "Do whatever my Son tells you." Enable us to *persevere with Christ.* Enable us, Mother of the Church, to *build up his Mystical Body* by living with the life that he alone can grant us from his fullness, which is both divine and human.

A Mhuire na nGrás, a Mháthair Mhic Dé,
Go gcuire tú ar mo leas mé.

"Rejoice in the Lord always."

"Máthair Dé, keep Ireland true to her spiritual tradition."

"You are also servants of your brothers and sisters."

"Help this land to stay true to you and your Son always."

Address to the sick, Knock

Dear brothers and sisters,

The Gospels are filled with instances where Our Lord shows his particular love and concern for the sick and for all those in pain. Jesus loved those who suffered, and this attitude has been passed on to his Church. To love the sick is something that the Church has learned from Christ.

Today I am happy to be with the sick and the handicapped. I have come to give witness to Christ's love for you, and to tell you that the Church and the Pope love you too. They reverence and esteem you. They are convinced that there is something very special about your mission in the Church.

By his suffering and death Jesus took on himself all human suffering, and he gave it a new value. As a matter of fact, he calls upon the sick, upon everyone who suffers, to collaborate with him in the salvation of the world.

Because of this, pain and sorrow are not endured alone or in vain. Although it remains difficult to understand suffering, Jesus has made it clear that its value is linked to his own suffering and death, to his own sacrifice. In other words, by your suffering you help Jesus in his work of salvation. This great truth is difficult to express accurately, but Saint Paul puts it this way: ". . . in my flesh I complete what is lacking in Christ's afflictions for the sake of his body, that is, the Church" (Col 1:24).

Your call to suffering requires strong faith and patience. Yes, it means that you are called to love with a special intensity. But remember that Our Blessed Mother, Mary, is close to you, just as she was close to Jesus at the foot of the cross. And she will never leave you all alone.

Address to handmaids and helpers at the Shrine and to directors of pilgrimages, Knock

 Dear brothers and sisters in the Lord,

As a pastor I feel in my heart a special joy in addressing a few words also to the handmaids and stewards of the Knock Shrine Society and to the directors of pilgrimages of Cnoc Mhuire, the Mountain of Mary.

The Eucharistic celebration of this afternoon brings back happy memories of the many pilgrimages in which I took part in my homeland at the Shrine of Jasna Góra, the Bright Mountain, in Czestochowa and at the other sites throughout Poland; it also recalls my visit to the Shrine of Our Lady of Guadalupe in Mexico.

I know from firsthand experience the value of the services you render to make every pilgrim feel at home at this Shrine, and to help them to make every visit a loving and prayerful encounter with Mary, the Mother of Divine Grace. In a special way, you are the servants of the Mother of Jesus. You help people to approach her, to receive her message of love and dedication, and to entrust to her their whole life so that they may be true witnesses to the love of her Son.

You are also servants of your brothers and sisters. In helping and guiding the many pilgrims and especially the sick and handicapped, you perform not only a work of charity but also a task of evangelisation. May this insight be your inspiration and your strength in order that all the tasks that you so generously accept to perform may become a living witness for the word of God and for the good tidings of salvation.

I pray for you, I thank you, and I invoke upon you abundant graces of goodness and holiness of life. Receive the blessing which I cordially extend to you and all your loved ones.

Maynooth

St Patrick's College, Maynooth, stands on a site which has had historical and Church associations with the Earls of Kildare since the thirteenth century. The castle there was the stronghold of Silken Thomas, from whom it was taken in a week-long siege by Lord Skeffington, Deputy of King Henry VIII, in 1535. During this event, the castle had the dubious distinction of being bombarded by the first siege guns to be used in Ireland.

The survivors of the siege were executed by Skeffington, despite a previous promise to spare them, resulting in a hated phrase — the pardons of Maynooth. A religious community had been founded there in 1521, but was suppressed by Henry VIII in 1538.

In 1795, a seminary was founded on the site by the English authorities because they feared the influence of the French Revolution on Irish priests then being educated in Paris. It became the greatest seminary in these islands (10,000 priests have been ordained there), sending priests to all parts of the world, including Britain, France, Australia, the USA and the Phillipines.

In 1896, it was granted the status of a Pontifical University, with faculties of philosophy, theology, and canon law. Twelve years later it became a recognised college of the newly-formed National University of Ireland, with faculties of arts, Celtic studies, philosophy, and science.

Many renovations were carried out in the nineteenth century, one of which was the Gothic quadrangle, designed by the English architect Augustus Welby Pugin. The college chapel designed by the Irish Gothic-Revival architect J.J. McCarthy, though he died before its completion.

The college has a small collection of antiquities and art, mainly ecclesiastical. It includes examples of electrical apparatus invented and used by Rev. Nicholas Callan, who was Professor of Science in the college from 1826 to 1864. Dr Callan was responsible for the invention of the step-up transformer and the discovery of the principle of the self-induced dynamo.

John Paul II signed the visitors book which contains the signatures of many other famous people, including Edward VII, Queen Alexandra, George V, Queen Mary, Princess Grace of Monaco, Karl Rahner, and a number of presidents of Ireland, including Eamon de Valera.

The Pope was presented with a specially bound *History of Maynooth* by Most Rev. John Healy and three bound volumes, in Polish of Walter Macken's books: *Seek the Fair Land, The Silent People,* and *The Scorching Wind in Polish.*

After his address, the Pope blessed the foundation stone of the new John Paul II Library. The foundation stone, of blue limestone donated by the community of the Cistercian monastery of Mount Melleray, Co. Waterford, bears the inscription (in Latin and in English):

> Pope John Paul II
> On the happy occasion of his presence in the College
> blessed this auspicious Library foundation stone
> on 1 October 1979.

Guests at Maynooth during the Pope's visit included representatives of the National University of Ireland, Kildare County Council, heads of major seminaries and houses of study in Ireland, James Galway, and the New Irish Chamber Orchestra.

Maynooth
   Attendance: 70,000
   Seminarists: 1,000
   Stewards: 400
   Gardaí: 400
   Medical personnel: 3 doctors, 10 nurses, 5 ambulances,
      1 fire tender

"You must work for the Lord with a sense of urgency."

"As far as the future goes, brethren, courage and trust." —CABRA

Address to seminarists, Maynooth

 Dear brothers and sons in Our Lord Jesus Christ,
You have a very special place in my heart and in the heart of the Church. During my visit to Maynooth I wanted to be alone with you, even though it could be for only a few moments.

I have many things that I would tell you — things that I have been saying about the life of seminarists and about seminaries all during the first year of my pontificate.

In particular I would like to speak again about the word of God: about how you are called to hear and guard and do the word of God. And about how you are to base your entire lives and ministry upon the word of God, just as it is transmitted by the Church, just as it is expounded by the Magisterium, just as it has been understood throughout the history of the Church by the faithful guided by the Holy Spirit: *semper et ubique et ab omnibus*. The word of God is the great treasure of your lives. Through the word of God you will come to a deep knowledge of the mystery of Jesus Christ, Son of God and son of Mary: Jesus Christ, the high priest of the New Testament and the Saviour of the World.

The word of God is worthy of all your efforts. To embrace it in its purity and integrity, and to spread it by word and example is a great mission. And this is your mission, today and tomorrow and for the rest of your lives.

As you pursue your vocation — a vocation so intimately related to the word of God, I wish to recall to you one simple but important lesson taken from the life of Saint Patrick, and it is this: in the history of evangelisation, the destiny of an entire people — your people — was radically affected for time and eternity because of the fidelity with which Saint Patrick embraced and proclaimed the word of God, and by reason of the fidelity with which Saint Patrick pursued his call to the end.

What I really want you to realise is this: that God counts on you; that he make his plans, in a way, depend on your free collaboration, on the oblation of your lives, and on the generosity with which you follow the inspirations of the Holy Spirit in the depths of your hearts.

The Catholic faith of Ireland today was linked, in God's plan, to the fidelity of Saint Patrick. And tomorrow, yes, tomorrow, some part of God's plan will be linked to your fidelity — to the fervour with which you say "Yes" to God's word in your lives.

Today, Jesus Christ is making this appeal to you through me: the appeal for fidelity. In prayer you will see more and more every day what I mean and what the implications of this call are. By God's grace you will understand more and more every day how God requires and accepts your fidelity as a condition for the supernatural effectiveness of all your activity. The supreme expression of fidelity will come with your irrevocable and total selfgiving in union with Jesus Christ to his Father. And may Our Blessed Mother, Mary, help you to make this gift acceptable.

Remember Saint Patrick. Remember what the fidelity of just one man has meant for Ireland and the world. Yes, dear sons and brothers, fidelity to Jesus Christ and to his word makes all the difference in the world. Let us therefore look up to Jesus, who is for all time the faithful witness of the Father.

"Christ looks on you and loves you."

Father,

In your plan for our salvation you
provide shepherds for your people.

Bring to fulfilment the good work
you have begun in these young men.

Raise them up as worthy ministers
for your altar and gentle servants
of your Gospel.

Through them may the compassion of
your Son, Jesus Christ, heal the wounds
of sin and division.

Amen.

Address to priests, missionaries, religious brothers and sisters, seminarists, Maynooth

Praised be Jesus Christ!

My dear brothers and sisters in Christ,

1. The name of Maynooth is respected all over the Catholic world. It recalls what is noblest in the Catholic priesthood in Ireland. Here come seminarists from every Irish diocese, sons of Catholic homes which were themselves true "seminaries", true seed-beds of priestly or religious vocations. From here have gone out priests to every Irish diocese and to the dioceses of the far-flung Irish diaspora. Maynooth has, in this century, given birth to two new missionary societies, one initially directed towards China, the other towards Africa; and it has sent out hundreds of alumni as volunteers to the mission fields. Maynooth is a school of priestly holiness, an academy of theological learning, a university of Catholic inspiration. Saint Patrick's College is a place of rich achievement, which promises a future just as great.

Therefore Maynooth is a fitting place in which to meet and talk with priests, diocesan and religious, with religious brothers, religious sisters, missionaries and seminarists. Having, as a priest-student in Paris, lived for a time in the atmosphere of an Irish seminary — the Collège Irlandais in Paris, now loaned by the Irish bishops to the hierarchy of Poland — I have profound joy in meeting with you all here in Ireland's national seminary.

2. My first words go to the priests, diocesan and religious. I say to you what Saint Paul said to Timothy. I ask you "to fan into a flame the gift that God gave you when (the bishop) laid (his) hands on you" (2 Tim 1:6). Jesus Christ himself, the one High Priest said: "I have come to bring fire to the earth, and how I wish it were blazing already!" (Lk 12:49). You share in his priesthood; you carry on his work in the world. His work cannot be done by lukewarm or half-hearted priests. His fire of love for the Father and for men must burn in you. His longing to save mankind must consume you.

You are called by Christ as the apostles were. You are appointed, like them, to be with Christ. You are sent, as they were, to go out in his name, and by his authority, to "make disciples of all the nations" (cf Mt 10:1; 28:19; Mk 3:13—16).

Your first duty is to be *with Christ*. You are each called to be "a witness to his Resurrection" (Acts 1:22). A constant danger with priests, even zealous priests, is that they become so immersed in the work of the Lord that they neglect the Lord of the work.

We must find time, we must make time, to be with the Lord in prayer. Following the example of the Lord Jesus himself, we must "always go off to some place where (we can) be alone and pray" (cf Lk 5:16). It is only if we spend time with the Lord that our sending out to others will be also a bringing of him to others.

3. To be with the Lord is always also to be sent by him to do his work. A priest is *called* by Christ; a priest is *with* Christ; a priest is *sent* by Christ. A priest is sent in the power of the same Holy Spirit which drove Jesus untiringly along the roads of life, the roads of history. Whatever the difficulties, the disappointments, the set-backs, we priests find in Christ and in the power of his Spirit the strength to "struggle wearily on, helped only by his power driving (us) irresistibly" (cf Col 1:29).

As priests, you are privileged to be pastors of a faithful people, who continue to respond generously to your ministry, and who are a strong support to your own priestly vocation through their faith and their prayer. If you keep striving to be the kind of priest your people expect and wish you to be, then you will be holy priests. The degree of religious practice in Ireland is high. For this we must be constantly thanking God. But will this high level of religious practice continue? Will the next generation of young Irish men and Irish women still be as faithful as their fathers were? After my two days in Ireland, after my meeting with Ireland's youth in Galway, I am confident that they will. But this will require both unremitting work and untiring prayer on your part. You must work for the Lord with a sense of urgency. You must work with the conviction that this generation, this decade of the 1980s which we are about to enter, could be crucial and decisive for the future of the faith in Ireland. Let there be no complacency. As Saint Paul said: "Be awake to all the dangers; stay firm in the faith; be brave and be strong" (1 Cor 16:13). Work with confidence; work with joy. You are witnesses to the resurrection of Christ.

4. What the people expect from you, more than anything else, is faithfulness to the priesthood. This is what speaks to them of the faithfulness of God. This is what strengthens them to be faithful to Christ through all the difficulties of their lives, of their marriages. In a world so marked by instability as our world today, we need more signs and witnesses to God's fidelity to us, and to the fidelity we owe to him. This is what causes such great sadness to the Church, such great but often silent anguish among the people of God, when priests fail in their fidelity to their priestly commitment. That counter-sign, that counter-witness, has been one of the set-backs to the great hopes for renewal aroused throughout the Church by the Second Vatican Council. Yet this has also driven priests, and the whole Church, to more intense and fervent prayer; for it has taught us all that without Christ we can do nothing (cf Jn 15:5). And the fidelity of the immense majority of priests has shone with even greater clarity and is all the more manifest and glorious a witness to the faithful God, and to Christ, the faithful witness (cf Rev 1:5).

5. In a centre of theological learning, which is also a seminary, like Maynooth, this witness of fidelity has the added importance and the special value of impressing on candidates for the priesthood the strength and the grandeur of priestly fidelity. Here in Maynooth, theological learning, being part of formation for the priesthood, is preserved from ever being an academic pursuit of the intellect only. Here theological scholarship is linked with liturgy, with prayer, with the building of a community of faith and love, and thus with the building up, the "edifying", of the priesthood of Ireland, and the edifying of the Church. My call today is a call to prayer. Only in prayer will we meet the challenges of our ministry and fulfil the hopes of tomorrow. All our appeals for peace and reconciliation can be effective only through prayer.

This theological learning, here as everywhere throughout the Church, is a reflection on faith, a reflection in faith. A theology which did not deepen faith and lead to prayer might be a discourse on words about God; it could not be a discourse about God, the

living God, the God who *is* and whose being is *love*. It follows that theology can only be authentic in the Church, the community of faith. Only when the teaching of theologians is in conformity with the teaching of the College of Bishops, united with the Pope, can the people of God know with certitude that that teaching is "the faith which has been once and for all entrusted to the Saints" (Jude 3). This is not a limitation for theologians, but a liberation; for it preserves them from subservience to changing fashions and binds them securely to the unchanging truth of Christ, the truth which makes us free (Jn 7:32).

6.   In Maynooth, in Ireland, to speak of priesthood is to speak of mission. Ireland has never forgotten that "the pilgrim Church is missionary by her very nature; for it is from the mission of the Son and the mission of the Holy Spirit that she takes her origin, in accordance with the decree of God the Father" (*Ad Gentes,* 2). In the ninth and tenth centuries, Irish monks rekindled the light of faith in regions where it had burnt low or been extinguished by the collapse of the Roman Empire, and evangelised new nations not yet evangelised, including areas of my own native Poland. How can I forget that there was an Irish monastery as far east as Kiev, even up to the thirteenth century; and that there was even an Irish college for a short time in my own city of Cracow, during the persecution of Cromwell. In the eighteenth and nineteenth centuries, Irish priests followed their exiles all over the English-speaking world. In the twentieth century, new missionary institutes of men and women sprang up in Ireland, which, together with the Irish branches of international missionary institutes and with existing Irish religious congregations, gave a new missionary impetus to the Church.

May that missionary spirit never decline in the hearts of Irish priests, whether members of missionary institutes or of the diocesan clergy or of religious congregations devoted to other apostolates. May this spirit be actively fostered by all of you among the laity, already so devoted in their prayer, so generous in their support for the missions. May a spirit of partnership grow between the home dioceses and the home religious congregations in the total mission of the Church, until each local diocesan Church and each religious congregation and community is fully seen to be "missionary of its very nature", entering into the eager missionary movement of the universal Church.

I have learned with much pleasure that the Irish Missionary Union plans to establish a national missionary centre, which will both serve as a focus for missionary renewal by missionaries themselves and foster the missionary awareness of the clergy, religious and faithful of the Irish Church. May its work be blessed by God. May it contribute to a great new upsurge of missionary fervour and a new wave of missionary vocations from this great motherland of faith which is Ireland.

7.   I wish to speak a special word to religious brothers. The past decade has brought great changes, and with them problems and trials unprecedented in all your previous experience. I ask you not to be discouraged. Be men of great truth, of great and unbounded hope. "May the God of Hope bring you such joy and peace in your faith that the power of the Holy Spirit will remove all bounds to hope" (Rom 15:13). The past decade has also brought a great renewal in your understanding of your holy vocation, a great deepening of your liturgical lives and your prayer, a great extension of the field of your apostolic influence. I ask God to bless you with renewed fidelity in vocation among your members, and with increased vocations to your institutes. The Church in Ireland and on the missions owes much to all the institutes of brothers. Your call to holiness is a precious adornment of the Church. Believe in your vocation. Be faithful to it. "God has called you and he will not fail you" (1 Thess 5:23).

8.   The sisters, too, have known years of searching, sometimes perhaps of uncertainty or of unrest. These have also been years of purification. I pray that we are now entering a period of consolidation and of construction. Many of you are engaged in the apostolate of education and the pastoral care of youth. Do not doubt the continuing relevance of that apostolate, particularly in modern Ireland, where youth are such a large and important part of the population. The Church has repeatedly, in many solemn recent documents, reminded religious of the primary importance of education, and has invited congregations of men and women with the tradition and the charism of education to persevere in that vocation and to redouble their commitment to it. The same is true of the traditional apostolates of care of the sick, nursing, care of the aged, the handicapped, the poor. These must not be neglected while new apostolates are being undertaken. In the words of the Gospel, you must "bring out from (your) storeroom things both new and old" (cf Mt 13:52). You must be courageous in your apostolic undertakings, not letting difficulties, shortage of personnel, insecurity for the future, deter or depress you.

But remember always that your field of apostolate is your own personal lives. Here is where the message of the Gospel has first to be preached and lived. Your first apostolic duty is your own sanctification. No change in religious life has any importance unless it be also conversion of yourselves to Christ. No movement in religious life has any value unless it be also movement inwards to the "still centre" of your existence, where Christ is. It is not what you *do* that matters most; but what you *are*, as women

consecrated to God. For you, Christ has consecrated himself, so that you too "may be consecrated in truth" (cf Jn 17:19).

To you and to priests, diocesan and religious, I say: Rejoice to be witnesses to Christ in the modern world. Do not hesitate to be recognisable, identifiable, in the streets as men and women who have consecrated their lives to God and who have given up everything worldly to follow Christ. Believe in the value for contemporary men and women of the visible signs of your consecrated lives. People need signs and reminders of God in the modern secular city, which has few reminders of God left. Do not help the trend towards "taking God off the streets" by adopting secular modes of dress and behaviour yourselves.

10.   My special blessing and greeting goes to the cloistered sisters and contemplatives, men as well as women. I express to you my gratitude for what you have done for me by your lives of prayer and sacrifice since my papal ministry began. I express the Pope's need for you, the Church's need for you. You are foremost in that "great, intense and growing prayer" for which I called in *Redemptor Hominis*. Never was the contemplative vocation more precious or relevant than in our modern restless world. May there be many Irish boys and girls called to the contemplative life, at this time when the future of the Church and the future of humanity depend on prayer.

Gladly do I repeat to all contemplatives, on this feast of Saint Thérèse of Lisieux, the words I used in addressing the sisters of Rome:

> I commend to you the Church; I commend mankind and the world to you. To you, to your prayers, to your "holocaust" I commend also myself, Bishop of Rome. Be with me, close to me, you who are in the heart of the Church! May there be fulfilled in each of you that which was the programme of life for Saint Theresa of the Child Jesus: "in corde Ecclesiae amor ero" – "I will be love in the heart of the Church"!

Much of what I have been saying has been intended also for the seminarists. You are preparing for the total giving of yourselves to Christ and to the service of his kingdom. You bring to Christ the gift of your youthful enthusiasm and vitality. In you Christ is eternally youthful; and through you he gives youth to the Church. Do not disappoint him. Do not disappoint the people who are waiting for you to bring Christ to them. Do not fail your generation of young Irish men and women. Bring Christ to the young people of your generation as the only answer to their longings. Christ looks on you and loves you. Do not, like the young man in the Gospel, go away sad, "because he had great possessions" (cf Mt 19:22). Instead, bring all your possessions of mind and hand and heart to Christ, that he may use them to "draw all men to himself" (cf Jn 12:32).

To all of you I say: this is a wonderful time in the history of the Church. This is a wonderful time to be a priest, to be a religious, to be a missionary for Christ. Rejoice in the Lord always. Rejoice in your vocation. I repeat to you the words of Saint Paul:

> I want you to be happy, always happy in the Lord; I repeat, what I want is your happiness. There is no need to worry; but if there is anything you need, pray for it, asking God for it with prayer and thanksgiving, and that peace of God which is so much greater than we can understand will guard your hearts and your thoughts, in Christ Jesus (Phil 4:4–7).

Mary, Mother of Christ, the Eternal Priest, Mother of priests and of religious, will keep you from all anxiety, as you "wait in joyful hope for the coming of our Lord and Saviour, Jesus Christ". Entrust yourselves to her, as I commend you to her, to Mary, Mother of Jesus and Mother of his Church.

'Brethren, let us go forward together for the ~ood of Ireland.'' – Nunciature

Limerick

Limerick today is the third largest city in the Republic of Ireland. The name in Irish "Luimneach" means "a bare spot", and it was here, in the ninth century, that the Danes built a fortress. Later they established a "Thing-motte" or Courthouse, and thus introduced Danish law and order among the original Irish Christian inhabitants.

The patron saint of the diocese of Limerick in St Munchin, who was one of the early abbots of Mungret. The most important ecclesiastical building from medieval times is St Mary's Cathedral, built at the end of the twelfth century in Gothic style. It is the Church of Ireland cathedral today. The Roman Catholic Cathedral of St John, in revived Gothic style, was designed by Thomas Hardwicke, and opened to the public in 1861.

Among the treasures of former times preserved in Limerick are the O'Dea Mitre and Crozier, dating from 1418, and the Bishop Arthur Chalice, 1625.

Still dominating the Limerick skyline and panorama is St John's Castle, built in 1210, lying beside Thomond Bridge on the river Shannon. Nearby, on the other side of Thomond Bridge, is the Treaty Stone, on which, according to tradition, the Treaty of Limerick was signed in 1691.

Limerick became famous in the 1920s on account of the Shannon Scheme, which was the largest hydo-electric scheme in Europe at the time, and which played such a large part in helping to industrialise modern Ireland.

In more recent years Limerick has been chosen as the site of the new third level educational experiment, the National Institute for Higher Education, in Plassy. The campus already has some thirteen hundred students, and also houses the National College of Physical Education.

Greenpark, where Pope John Paul II was received in Limerick, covers an area of some 135 acres, and has been Limerick Race Course since 1890. The grandstand was erected in 1893.

The Treaty Stone

Limerick
  Attendance: 400,000
  Concelebrants: 26 (11 bishops, 2 abbots, 13 priests)
  Communion priests: 800
  Communicants: 200,000
  Choir: 150
  Stewards: 1,600
  Army: 300
  Civil Defence: 200
  Scouts: 600
  Gifts offered: a rosary beads; old prayer-book, set in sere and yellow leaves with evergreens, presented by older people; Dromcollogher Bell (Dresden); Stations of the Cross; St Brigid's Cross; a bound copy of Fintan O'Carroll's *Mass;* Waterford Glass cruets; paten, handmade in Glenstal; Bishop Arthur Chalice (1625); catechism, set in flowers, presented by children

Homily at the Mass for the People of God, Limerick

A phobail dhílis na Mumhan, go mbeannaí Dia dhíbh.

Dear brothers and sisters in Christ,

1.   On this last day of my visit to Ireland I come to you to celebrate with you the Holy Eucharist. I wish to seal once more, in the love of Christ Jesus, the bond that links the successor of Peter in the See of Rome with the Church that is in Ireland. In you I greet once more all the people of Ireland, who have taken their place in the mystery of the Church through the preaching of Saint Patrick and through the sacraments of baptism and confirmation. I invite you to make this last Mass, which I offer with you and for you, into a special hymn of thanksgiving to the Most Holy Trinity for the days that I have been able to spend in your midst.

I come in the name of Christ to preach to you his own message. The liturgy of the word today speaks of a building, of the cornerstone that supports and gives strength to the house, of the city that is built on the hill for security and protection. These images contain an invitation for all of us, for all Christians, to come close to Christ, the cornerstone, so that he may become our support and the unifying principle which gives meaning and coherence to our lives. It is the same Christ who gives dignity to all the members of the Church and who assigns to each one his mission.

2.   Today, I would like to speak to you about that special dignity and mission entrusted to the lay people in the Church. Saint Peter says that Christians are "a royal priesthood, a holy nation" (1 Pet 2:9). All Christians, incorporated into Christ and his Church by baptism, are consecrated to God. They are called to profess the faith which they have received. By the sacrament of confirmation, they are further endowed by the Holy Spirit with special strength to be witnesses of Christ and sharers in his mission of salvation. Every lay Christian is therefore an extraordinary work of God's grace and is called to the heights of holiness. Sometimes, lay men and women do not seem to appreciate to the full the dignity and the vocation that is theirs as lay people. No, there is no such thing as an "ordinary layman", for all of you have been called to conversion through the death and resurrection of Jesus Christ. As God's holy people you are called to fulfill your rôle in the evangelisation of the world.

Yes, the laity are "a chosen race, a holy priesthood", also called to be "the salt of the earth" and "the light of the world". It is their specific vocation and mission to express the Gospel in their lives and thereby to insert the Gospel as a leaven into the reality of the world in which they live and work. The great forces which shape the world — politics, the mass media, science, technology, culture, education, industry and work — are precisely the areas where lay people are especially competent to exercise their mission. If these forces are guided by people who are true disciples of Christ, and who are, at the same time, fully competent in the relevant secular knowledge and skill, then indeed will the world be transformed from within by Christ's redeeming power.

3.   Lay people today are called to a strong Christian commitment, to permeate society with the leaven of the Gospel, for Ireland is at a point of decision in her history. The Irish people have to choose today their way forward. Will it be the transformation of

all strata of humanity into a new creation, or the way that many nations have gone, giving excessive importance to economic growth and material possessions, while neglecting the things of the spirit? The way of preferring economic growth and material possession to the things of the spirit? The way of substituting a new ethic of temporal enjoyment for the law of God? The way of false freedom which is only slavery to decadence? Will it be the way of subjugating the dignity of the human person to the totalitarian domination of the State? The way of violent struggle between classes? The way of extolling revolution over God?

Ireland must choose. You, the present generation of Irish people, must decide; your choice must be clear and your decision firm. Let the voice of your forefathers, who suffered so much to maintain their faith in Christ and thus to preserve Ireland's soul, resound today in your ears through the voice of the Pope when he repeats the words of Christ: "What will it profit a man, if he gains the whole world, and forfeits his life?" (Mt 16:26). What would it profit Ireland to go the easy way of the world and suffer the loss of her own soul?

Your country seems in a sense to be living again the temptations of Christ: Ireland is being asked to prefer the "kingdoms of the world and their splendour" to the kingdom of God (cf Mt 4:8). Satan, the tempter, the adversary of Christ, will use all his might and all his deceptions to win Ireland for the way of the world. What a victory he would gain, what a blow he would inflict on the Body of Christ in the world, if he could seduce Irish men and women away from Christ. Now is the time of testing for Ireland. This generation is once more a generation of decision.

Dear sons and daughters of Ireland, pray, pray not to be led into temptation. I asked in my first encyclical for a "great, intense and growing prayer for all the Church". I ask you today for a great, intense and growing prayer for all the people of Ireland, for the Church in Ireland, for all the Church which owes so much to Ireland. Pray that Ireland may not fail in the test. Pray as Jesus taught us to pray: "Lead us not into temptation, but deliver us from evil."

Above all, have an immense confidence in the merits of Our Lord Jesus Christ and in the power of his death and resurrection. It is precisely because of the strength of his paschal mystery that each of us and all Ireland can say: "I can do all things in him who strengthens me" (Phil 4:13).

4. Ireland in the past displayed a remarkable interpenetration of her whole culture, speech and way of life by the things of God and the life of grace. Life was in a sense organised around religious events. The task of this generation of Irish men and women is to transform the more complex world of modern industrial and urban life by the same Gospel spirit. Today, you must keep the city and the factory for God, as you have always kept the farm and the village community for him in the past. Material progress has in so many place led to decline of faith and growth in Christ, growth in love and justice.

To accomplish this you must have, as I said in Phoenix Park, consistency between your faith and your daily life. You cannot be a genuine Christian on Sunday, unless you try to be true to Christ's spirit also in your work, your commercial dealings, at your trade union or your employers' or professional meetings. How can you be a true community in Christ at Mass unless you try to think of the welfare of the whole national community when decisions are being taken by your particular sector or group? How can you be ready to meet Christ in judgement unless you remember how the poor

are affected by the behaviour of your group or by your personal life style? For Christ will say to us all: "In so far as you did this to one of the least of these brothers of mine, you did it to me" (Mt 25:40).

I have learned with great joy and gratitude of the wonderful spirit of work and cooperation with which you all joined in the material preparations as well as the spiritual preparation for this papal visit. How much more wonderful still it would be if you could have the same spirit of work and cooperation always "for the glory of God and the honour of Ireland"!

5.   Here in Limerick, I am in a largely rural area and many of you are people of the land. I feel at home with you as I did with the rural and mountain people of my native Poland, and I repeat here to you what I told them: love the land, love the work of the fields for it keeps you close to God, the creator, in a special way.

To those who have gone to the cities, here or abroad, I say: keep in contact with your roots in the soil of Ireland, with your families and your culture. Keep true to the faith, to the prayers and the values you learned here; and pass on that heritage to your children, for it is rich and good.

To all I say, revere and protect your family and your family life, for the family is the primary field of Christian action for the Irish laity, the place where your "royal priesthood" is chiefly exercised. The Christian family has been in the past Ireland's greatest spiritual resource. Modern conditions and social changes have created new patterns and new difficulties for family life and for Christian marriage. I want to say to you: do not be discouraged, do not follow the trends where a close-knit family is seen as outdated; the Christian family is more important for the Church and for society today than ever before.

It is true that the stability and sanctity of marriage are being threatened by new ideas and by the aspirations of some. Divorce, for whatever reason it is introduced, inevitably becomes easier and easier to obtain and it gradually comes to be accepted as a normal part of life. The very possibility of divorce in the sphere of civil law makes stable and permanent marriages more difficult for everyone. May Ireland always continue to give witness before the modern world to her traditional commitment, corresponding to the true dignity of man, to the sanctity and the indissolubility of the marriage bond. May the Irish always support marriage, through personal commitment and through positive social and legal action.

Above all, hold high the esteem for the wonderful dignity and grace of the sacrament of marriage. Prepare earnestly for it. Believe in the spiritual power which this sacrament of Jesus Christ gives to strengthen the marriage union, and to overcome all the crises and problems of life together. Married people must believe in the power of the sacrament to make them holy; they must believe in their vocation to witness through their marriage to the power of Christ's love. True love and the grace of God can never let marriage become a self-centered relationship of two individuals, living side by side for their own interests.

6.   And here, I want to say a very special word to all Irish parents. Marriage must include openness to the gift of children. Generous openness to accept children from God as the gift to their love is the mark of the Christian couple. Respect the God-given cycle of life, for this respect is part of our respect for God himself, who created male and female, who created them in his own image, reflecting his own life-giving love in the patterns of their sexual being.

And so I say to all, have an absolute and holy respect for the sacredness of human life from the first moment of its conception. Abortion, as the Vatican Council stated, is one of the "abominable crimes" (*Gaudium et Spes,* 51). To attack unborn life at any moment from its conception is to undermine the whole moral order which is the true guardian of the well-being of man. The defence of the absolute inviolability of unborn life is part of the defence of human rights and human dignity. May Ireland never weaken in her witness, before Europe and before the whole world, to the dignity and sacredness of all human life, from conception until death.

Dear fathers and mothers of Ireland, believe in your vocation, that beautiful vocation of marriage and parenthood which God has given to you. Believe that God is with you — for all parenthood in heaven and on earth takes its name from him. Do not think that anything you will do in life is more important than to be a good Christian father and mother. May Irish mothers, young women and girls not listen to those who tell them that working at a secular job, succeeding in a secular profession, is more important than the vocation of giving life and caring for this life as a mother. The future of the Church, the future of humanity depend in great part on parents and on the family life that they build in their homes. The family is the true measure of the greatness of a nation, just as the dignity of man is the true measure of civilisation.

7.   Your homes should always remain homes of prayer. As I leave today this island which is so dear to my heart, this land and its people which is such a consolation and strength to the Pope, may I express a wish: that every home in Ireland may remain or may begin again to be, a home of daily family prayer. That you would promise me to do this would be the greatest gift you could give me as I leave your hospitable shores.

I know that your bishops are preparing a pastoral programme designed to encourage greater sharing by parents in the religious education of their children under the motto "handing on the faith in the home". I am confident that you will all join in this programme with enthusiasm and generosity. To hand on to your children the faith you received from your parents is your first duty and your greatest privilege as parents. The home should be the first school of religion, as it must be the first school of prayer. The great spiritual influence of Ireland in the history of the world was due in great degree to the religion of the homes of Ireland, for here is where evangelisation begins, here is where vocations are nurtured. I appeal therefore to Irish parents to continue fostering vocations to the priesthood and the religious life in their homes, among their sons and daughters. It was, for generations, the greatest desire of every Irish parent to have a son a priest or religious, to have a daughter consecrated to God. May it continue to be your desire and your prayer. May increased opportunities for boys and girls never lessen your esteem for the privilege of having a son or daughter of yours selected by Christ and called by him to give up all things and follow him.

I entrust all this to Mary, bright "Sun of the Irish race". May her prayers help all Irish homes to be like the holy house of Nazareth. From them may all Christians go forth, as Jesus did from Nazareth. May they go forth in the power of the Spirit to continue Christ's work and to follow in his footsteps towards the end of the millennium, into the twenty-first century. Mary will keep you all close to him, who is "Father of the world to come" (Is 9:6).

Dia agus Muire libh!
May God and Mary be with you and with the families of Ireland, always!
Slán go deo le brón is buairt, agus beannacht Dé libh go léir.

Greeting to the President of Ireland, Dr P. J. Hillery, Dublin

Mr President,

I wish to express my gratitude for the warm welcome that I have received on my arrival in Ireland from the people of Ireland, as well as from their distinguished representatives. I express my sincere thanks to you, Mr President, for the kind words that you addressed to me, with which you have wished to honour not only my person but the Head of the Roman Catholic Church.

It was fitting after my visit to Latin America and to my beloved homeland, that I should accept the invitation of the Irish Episcopate to come to your Emerald Isle and meet your people. Many are indeed the bonds that unite your country to the See of Peter in Rome. From the earliest beginnings of Christianity in this land, all through the centuries until the present day, never has the love of the Irish for the Vicar of Christ been weakened, but it has flourished as an example for all to witness. In receiving the faith from Saint Patrick, the Irish Catholic people have also accepted that the Church of Christ is built on the Rock that is Peter, and they have established that loving relationship with the successors of Saint Peter that has always been a guarantee for the preservation of their faith. It gives me pleasure to state here that this unfailing loyalty has been matched only by their profound devotion to Our Blessed Lady and by their steadfast fidelity to the duties of religion.

The history of Ireland has certainly not been without its share of suffering and pain. Economic and social conditions have induced many of her sons and daughters in the past to leave home and family and to seek elsewhere the opportunities for life in dignity that were not to be found here. Their loss for Ireland has been a gain for the countries where they settled. Those who remained have not always enjoyed a progress without setbacks. But through it all, the Irish have displayed an uncommon courage and perseverance inspired by their faith. May I be allowed, Mr President, to quote here from your last Saint Patrick's Day message, where you credit your patron saint for "the moral fibre and spiritual wealth that sustained our nation in times of trial".

My fervent wish for you and your fellow Irish men and women is that those same qualities — heritage of a living faith preserved and deepened through the centuries — may enable this country to move towards the third millennium and to achieve a well-being that constitutes a true human advancement for all your people, a well-being that brings honour to the name and the history of Ireland. The vitality that draws its strength from over fifteen centuries of uninterrupted Christian tradition will enable you to tackle the many problems of a modern and still young republic.

The elimination of poverty, the uplifting of the deprived, the finding of full employment for all and especially for the very large number of splendid young people with whom God has blessed your country at this time, the creation of social and economic well-being for all classes of society remain real challenges. Reaching the goals of justice in the economic and social fields will require that religious convictions and fervour be not separated from a moral and social conscience, especially for those who plan and control the economic process, be they legislators, government officials, industrialists, trade unionists, office workers or manual workers.

The part that your nation has played with prominence and distinction in the history of Europe, on the spiritual and cultural level, will inspire you also in the future, to make your own distinctive contribution to the growing unity of the European continent, preserving at the same time the values that characterise your community, and witnessing for them in the midst of the political, economic, social and cultural currents that flow through Europe in these days.

It is my fervent wish that this same Ireland will also continue, as it has in the past, to be a force for understanding, brotherhood and collaboration among all the nations of the world. Many of your fellow men and women are working already in every part of the world — and I mention here with special gratitude your many missionaries — bringing through their labours and their zeal, through their unpretentious and unselfish dedication, the assistance that so many of our brothers and sisters in other parts of the world need to advance in their own development and to be able to satisfy their basic needs.

Irish exiles and Irish missionaries have gone all over the world, and wherever they have gone they have made the name of Ireland loved and honoured. The history of Ireland has been and is a source of human and spiritual inspiration to people everywhere. Ireland has inherited a noble Christian and human mission and her contribution to the well-being of the world and to the shaping of a new Europe can be as great today as it was in the greatest days of Ireland's history. That is the mission, that is the challenge facing Ireland in this generation.

Finally, Mr President, I want to make a plea for peace and harmony for all the people of this island. Your sadness for the continued unrest, injustice, and violence in Northern Ireland is also my personal sadness and sorrow. On the occasion of the feast of Saint Patrick in 1972, my beloved and revered predecessor, Pope Paul VI, whose love for Ireland will always be remembered with gratitude, wrote to the late Cardinal William Conway:

> The Christian faith must convince all concerned that violence is not an acceptable solution to the problems of Ireland. But at the same time, the Christian sense of values convinces man that lasting peace can be built only on the firm foundation of justice.

Those words retain their full meaning today.
I thank you once again for your courteous and warm reception.
I lovingly bless you, your land and your people.
Dia is Muire libh.
Beannacht Dé is Muire libh.
May God and Mary be with you.
May the blessing of God amd the blessing of Mary be with you and with the people of Ireland always.

Address to the Diplomatic Corps, Dublin

Your Excellencies, members of the Diplomatic Corps,

It give me great pleasure to have this meeting with you on my first day in Ireland. I greatly appreciate your warm welcome and I cordially thank the distinguished Dean of the Diplomatic Corps for the words which he so eloquently addressed to me. I accept these words as the expression of your esteem for the mission of the Apostolic See.

The pastoral journey that I began today has a deep meaning for me for several reasons, which I would like to share with you. As successor of Peter in the See of Rome, I have been entrusted with a particular care for the universal Church and for all her members. After my visit to Mexico, where the Third General Assembly of the Bishops of Latin America called me, and after my participation in the ceremonies in Poland commemorating Saint Stanislaus, it was fitting for me to come also to this island, where the Christian faith and the bond of unity with the See of Peter have been kept unbroken from the very first moment of evangelisation to this day.

Saint Patrick not only was the first Primate of Ireland, but he also was the one who succeeded in implanting a religious tradition in the Irish soul, in such a way that all Irish Christians can rightly glory in the heritage of Saint Patrick. He was truly Irish, he was truly Christian: and the Irish people have preserved this same heritage of his through many centuries of challenges, suffering, and social and political upheavals, thereby setting an example for all who believe that the message of Christ enhances and strengthens the most profound aspirations of people for dignity, fraternal unity and truth. I have come to encourage the Irish people in their adherence to the message of Christ.

I intend by my visit to pay homage also to the rôle which the Church in Ireland has played in the evangelisation of the whole European continent. Christianity in Europe cannot be contemplated without reference to the wonderful work of the Irish missionaries and monks. This work is at the basis of many flourishing Christian communities all over the continent. I believe that the values which are so deeply embedded in the history and the culture of this people constitute a lasting force for the building up of a Europe where the spiritual dimension of man and of society remains the only guarantee for unity and progress.

As visible head of the Catholic Church and servant of humanity, I have come to an island that is marked by profound problems in relation to the situation in Northern Ireland. As I had the opportunity to state earlier today at Drogheda, it was my sincere and firm desire to proclaim personally a message of peace and reconciliation to the people in Northern Ireland, but circumstances have not permitted this. I have therefore spoken to them from Drogheda, reaffirming that the Christian sense of values must convince everyone that violence is never an acceptable solution for human problems and that true peace must be built on justice. I have called for reconciliation in the name of Christ.

I am also on my way to the United Nations, where I have been invited to address the General Assembly. My predecessors in the See of Peter have consistently expressed their esteem and encouragement for this organisation which constitutes the appropriate forum where all nations can meet in order to seek together the answers to the many problems of today's world. I go there as a messenger of peace, justice and truth, and I wish to express gratitude to all who devote themselves to international collaboration in order to create a secure and peaceful future for humanity.

The international visit which I begin today in Ireland and which I shall conclude on 7 October in the capital of the United States of America, will, I hope, be accompanied by the prayers of all believers and by the support of all men and women of good will.

Once again I express my gratitude for your presence here, and I pray that almighty God will bless you and your families with abundant grace, and sustain you in your important work for humanity.

Address to the Irish Government, Dublin

Mr Taoiseach,
I am very pleased that I can meet here with the members of the Irish government. You represent the aspirations, needs and future of the Irish people, but also their potential and the promises of the future that are contained in the past history of your country. The people of Ireland have had a long history of suffering and struggle to achieve their own cohesion as a modern State and to attain the measure of well-being that is due to every nation.

It is your privilege to serve the people, in their name and for their progress, through the mandate that the people have conferred on you. But there are also principles and imperatives that are of a higher order and without which no society can ever hope to foster the true common good. I do not need to spell out before you the demands of justice, of peaceful living in society, of respect and protection for the dignity that derives from the very nature and destiny of every human being as a creature of God's love. It is your task to embody in concrete and practical measures the collaboration of all the citizens towards these lofty goals.

An Ireland that is prosperous, peaceful and committed to the ideal of fraternal relations among its people is also a factor that will contribute to the peaceful and just future of Europe and the whole family of nations. Today at Drogheda, I have made a solemn and passionate plea for justice, for peace and for reconciliation, particularly with regard to the situation in Northern Ireland that can leave no Irishman, no Christian, and certainly not the Pope, indifferent. It is my fervent prayer that all the people of this island will display the courage and find the ways for resolving a problem that is not religious in nature, but that finds its origin in a variety of historical, social, economic and political reasons.

I desire to renew once again my cordial thanks to you for your kind welcome and for all that the public authorities have done to facilitate my pastoral visit to your country. I express my esteem for you and your colleagues in the government. May each one, according to the office and the dignity that he holds, discharge his duties inspired by a true desire to foster peace, justice and the respect of the human person.

Greeting to the visiting bishops, Dublin

Dear Brothers in Our Lord Jesus Christ,

That so many of you have come from different countries, to share with me the various moments of my visit, is a tribute both to Ireland and to yourselves, for it proves that you feel united with the Bishop of Rome in his "solicitude for all the Churches" (2 Cor 11:28), and at the same time it shows that you want to honour the faith of the Church in Ireland.

For is it not true that the Christian communities you represent have to discharge a duty of gratitude to the Church of Ireland? You who come from other European nations feel a particular relationship with the people that brought forth so many and so great missionaries, who in centuries past travelled untiringly across the mountains and rivers and through the plains of Europe to support the faith when it was flagging, to revive the Christian communities, and preach the word of the Lord. The vitality of the Church in Ireland made the establishing of many of your own communities possible. *Peregrinari pro Christo:* to be a voyager, a pilgrim for Christ, was their reason for leaving their dear native land; and the Church in Europe was given new life by their journeyings.

Outside the continent, Irish immigrants, priests and missionaries were again the founders of new dioceses and parishes, the builders of churches and schools, and their faith succeeded, sometimes against overwhelming odds, to bring Christ to new

regions and to imbue new communities with the same undivided love for Jesus and his mother, and with the same loyalty and affection for the Apostolic See in Rome as they had known in their homeland.

As we reflect on these historical realities, and as we witness together, during this visit, the piety, the faith and the vitality of the Irish Church, we cannot but feel blessed for these moments. Your presence here will in turn be an encouragement for the Irish episcopate and for the Irish Christians since, in seeing you gathered around the Bishop of Rome, they will see that it is the whole *Collegium Episcopale* that offers support to the local pastors and assumes its share of responsibility for the Church that is in Ireland. Let your love for Ireland and your appreciation of Ireland's place in the Church be expressed in prayer for a speedy return to peace in this beautiful island. Lead your faithful people in this earnest and untiring prayer to the Prince of Peace, through the intercession of Mary, Queen of Peace.

When the people of this beloved country see you, gathered together with the Irish bishops around the Bishop of Rome, they witness that special union that constitutes a core of the episcopal collegiality, a union of mind and heart, a union of commitment and dedication in the building up of the Body of Christ, that is the Church. It is this profound union, this sincere "communion", that confers depth and meaning to the concept of collegiality and that carries it beyond a mere practical collaboration or a sharing of insights. It then becomes a bond that truly unites the bishops of the whole world with the successor of Peter and among themselves, in order to carry out *cum Petro et sub Petro* the apostolic ministry which the Lord entrusted to the Twelve. Knowing that such are the sentiments that animate your presence here with me not only gives me satisfaction but also supports me in my own unique and universal pastoral ministry.

From this union among all the bishops will flow forth for each ecclesial community, and for the Church as a whole, abundant fruits of unity and communion among all the faithful and with their bishops, as well as with the visible head of the universal Church.

Thank you for sharing with me the privilege and the supernatural grace of this visit. May the Lord Jesus bless you and your dioceses with ever more abundant fruits of union in mind and heart. And may every Christian everywhere, and the whole Church of God as one, increasingly become a sign and a presence of hope for all of humanity.

"Let no one ever doubt the commitment of the Catholic Church . . . to the pursuit of the unity of Christians."

Address to the ecumenical meeting, Dublin

 My dear brothers in Christ,

Permit me to greet you in the love of our common Lord and Saviour, and with the words of his servant and apostle Paul: "Grace to you and peace from God our Father and the Lord Jesus Christ" (Eph 1:2).

I am happy to have the opportunity to come together with you in the holy name of Jesus and pray with you. For all of us here today the great promise contained in the Gospel is truly encouraging and uplifting: "For where two or three are gathered in my name, there am I in the midst of them" (Mt 18:20). And so we rejoice exceedingly to know that Jesus Christ is with us.

We know that he is near to us with the power of his paschal mystery, and that from his paschal mystery we draw light and strength to walk in what Saint Paul calls "the newness of life" (Rom 6:4).

What a great grace it is for the entire Christian world that, in this our day, the Holy Spirit has powerfully stirred up in human hearts a real desire for this "newness of life". And what a great gift of God it is that there exists today among Christians a deeper realisation of the need to be perfectly one in Christ and in his Church: to be one, in accordance with Christ's own prayer, even as he and his Father are one (cf Jn 17).

Our desire for Christian unity springs from a need to be faithful to the will of God, as revealed in Christ. Our unity in Christ, moreover, conditions the effectiveness of our evangelisation; it determines the credibility of our witness before the world. Christ prayed for the unity of his disciples, precisely "so that the world may believe . . ." (Jn 17:21).

Today has indeed been a memorable day in my life: to have embraced in the love of Christ my separated Christian brethren and to confess with them "that Jesus Christ is the Son of God" (1 Jn 4:15); that he is "the Saviour of all men" (1 Tim 5:10); that he is "the one Mediator between God and men, the man Christ Jesus" (1 Tim 2:5). From Drogheda this morning I appealed for peace and reconciliation according to the supreme will of Christ, who alone can unify the hearts of men in brotherhood and common witness.

Let no one ever doubt the commitment of the Catholic Church and of the Apostolic See of Rome to the pursuit of the unity of Christians. Last November, when I met the members of the Secretariat for Promoting Christian Unity, I spoke of the "intolerable scandal of division between Christians". I said that the movement towards unity must not stop until it has reached its goal; and I called for an energetic commitment by Catholic bishops, priests and people to forward this movement. I said on that occasion:

> The Catholic Church, faithful to the direction taken at the Council, not only wants to go forward on the way that leads to the restoration of unity, but is anxious, according to its means and in full submission to the promptings of the Holy Spirit, to strengthen at every level its contribution to this great movement of all Christians (Address of 18 November 1978).

I renew that commitment and that pledge today here in Ireland, where reconciliation between Christians takes on a special urgency, but where it also has special resources in the tradition of Christian faith and fidelity to religion which marks the Catholic and Protestant communities.

The work of reconciliation, the road to unity, may be long and difficult. But, as on the way to Emmaus, the Lord himself is with us on the way, always making "as if to go on" (Lk 24:28). He will stay with us until the longed-for moment comes, when we can join together in recognising him in the holy scriptures and "in the breaking of the bread" (Lk 24:35).

Meanwhile, the internal renewal of the Catholic Church, in total fidelity to the Second Vatican Council, to which I pledged all my energies at the beginning of my papal ministry, must continue with undiminished vigour. This renewal is itself an indispensable contribution to the work of unity between Christians. As we each, in our respective Churches, grow in our searching of the holy scriptures, in our fidelity to and continuity with the age-old tradition of the Christian Church, in our search for holiness and for authenticity of Christian living, we shall also be coming closer to Christ, and therefore closer to one another in Christ.

It is he alone, through the action of his Holy Spirit, who can bring our hopes to fulfilment. In him we place all our trust: in "Jesus Christ our hope" (1 Tim 1:2). Despite our human weakness and our sins, despite all obstacles, we accept in humility and faith the great principle enunciated by our Saviour: "What is impossible with men is possible with God" (Lk 18:27).

May this day truly mark, for all of us and for those whom we serve in Christ, the occasion for ever greater fidelity, in prayer and penance, to the cause of Jesus Christ, and to his message of truth and love, of justice and peace. May our common esteem and love for the holy and inspired word of God unite us ever more, as we continue to study and examine together the important issues affecting ecclesial unity in all its aspects, as well as the necessity for a united service to a world in need.

Ireland, dear brothers in Christ, has special and urgent need for the united service of Christians. All Irish Christians must stand together to defend spiritual and moral values against the inroads of materialism and moral permissiveness. Christians must unite together to promote justice and defend the rights and dignity of every human person. All Christians in Ireland must join together in opposing all violence and all assaults against the human person — from whatever quarter they come — and in finding Christian answers to the grave problems of Northern Ireland. We must all be ministers of reconciliation. We must by example as well as by word try to move citizens, communities and politicians towards the ways of tolerance, cooperation and love. No fear of criticism, no risk of resentment, must deter us from this task. The charity of Christ compels us. Precisely because we have one common Lord, Jesus Christ, we must accept together the responsibility of the vocation we have received from him.

Dear brothers: with a conviction linked to our faith, we realise that the destiny of the world is at stake, because the credibility of the Gospel has been challenged. Only in perfect unity can we Christians adequately give witness to the truth. And so our fidelity to Jesus Christ urges us to do more, to pray more, to love more.

May Christ the Good Shepherd show us how to lead our people along the path of love to the goal of perfect unity: for the praise and glory of the Father, and of the Son, and of the Holy Spirit. Amen.

Address to journalists, Dublin

 My friends of the communications media,
During my visit to Ireland, I wish to leave a special thought for all of you, a special word for each of you, so that in time to come you will remember: the Pope said many things to many people during his pastoral visit to Ireland, but this was his message to me.

That message is the second of the two great commandments of Jesus: "Love your neighbour as yourself." That message and that mandate should have a special meaning for you because your work makes you an honoured guest in millions of homes throughout the world.

Wherever the sounds of transmissions are heard, wherever the images you capture are seen, wherever the words you report are read, *there* is your neighbour. *There* is a person you must love, someone for whose total well-being you must work — and even sometimes go without sleep and miss your meals. You are the instruments through whom that person — and millions of others — enjoys a wider experience and is helped to become a more effective member of the world community, a true neighbour to others.

Your profession, by its very nature, makes you servants, willing servants, of the community. Many of the members of that community will differ from you in political views, in material prospects, in religious conviction or in moral performance. As good communicators, you serve them all just the same — with love and with truth; indeed with a love of truth. As good communicators, you build bridges to unite, not walls to divide. As good communicators, you work out of the conviction that love and service of neighbour are the most important business in your lives.

All your concern, then, will be for the community's good. You will feed it on the truth. You will enlighten its conscience and serve as its peacemaker. You will set before the community standards that will keep it stretching for a way of life and a mode of behaviour worthy of its potential, worthy of human dignity.

You will inspire the community, fire its ideals, stimulate its imagination — if necessary, taunt it — into getting the best out of itself, the human best, the Christian best. You will neither yield to any inducement nor bend before any threat which might seek to deflect you from total integrity in your professional service of those who are not only your neighbours, but your brothers and sisters in the family of God, the Father of us all.

You think of yourselves as hard-headed realists, and I am well aware of the realities with which you must contend. Yet this is the Pope's word to you. It is no small thing he asks, no mean challenge he leaves with you. What he challenges you to do is to build, here in the Irish community and in the world community, the kingdom of God, the kingdom of love and of peace.

I thank you all sincerely for the work you are doing in the coverage of this visit. I ask you to bring my thanks and my love to your families, as I pray for you and for them in the beautiful Irish formula: May God hold you in the hollow of his hand. May he keep you and your dear ones in his peace."

Broadcast to the sick
on RTE radio and television, Dublin

Dear brothers and sisters,
The purpose of my visit to Ireland is to proclaim the message of love and peace of Our Lord and Saviour Jesus Christ.

I would like to be able to embrace each person, to meet each group, to speak to everyone about the wonderful works of God. In particular, I would like to be able to talk individually to the sick, to the young and to the old, to those who are bedridden, to the handicapped, to everybody who, in one way or another, is carrying the burden of suffering, especially to those who are suffering as a result of violence.

Not all of you can leave your homes or hospitals and come to meet me. But all of you are in my thoughts and prayers. I am spiritually close to all of you, because you belong to Christ; and I am coming to represent Christ, to console you in his name, and to remind you of his love for you.

Although I cannot take away your suffering and your pain, I can assure you, in the name of the Lord, how important a contribution you can make to the Church, to the kingdom of God. When your patience and pain are united with the suffering of Christ, when they are accepted out of love, then they take on a value they never had before. They help in bringing salvation and holiness to the world. Suffering is difficult. Only love can make it easy, and perfect love can make it a joy.

Dear brothers and sisters: Our Lord Jesus Christ has given you a special task for the glory of his name. The Church esteems you and thanks you for your important contribution to the Gospel. I assure you that your sufferings have a purpose, an immense value in the eyes of God, and I need the continued support of your prayers.

I love you all and bless you. My blessing goes also to all those who are caring for you, the doctors, the nurses and the religious sisters and brothers who spend themselves assisting you in carrying your cross of suffering, to the chaplains who bring you the healing power of Christ, and to all the hospital staffs for their hidden and generous service.

From my heart I bless you all, in the name of the Father, and of the Son and of the Holy Spirit. Amen.

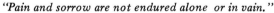

"Pain and sorrow are not endured alone or in vain."

Address to the Polish community, Dublin

Beloved fellow countrymen!

I would like to greet all of you who have come mainly from all over England to this meeting of ours that has been included in the programme of my visit to Ireland. The first year of my pontificate urges me for the third time to leave Rome — this time to go to Ireland and to the United States of America. The special motive for my journey is the invitation of the Secretary-General of the United Nations Organisation in New York, which I could not have left unanswered.

My visit to Ireland at the beginning of this responsible journey has a special meaning. I wish to express my thanks to all here present for your fraternal solidarity with the Pope, whose homeland is also yours. I am aware that this solidarity has been proved by your constant prayer and other spiritual acts supporting me in all my services. For my high mission I need this support immensely.

At the same time I would like to wish you all God's blessings in the lives that you live in Great Britain, while being still deeply rooted in Polish soil, in Polish culture and in Polish traditions. It is from Poland that you have brought over your faith, a bond of spiritual unity with the Bishop of Rome and with the whole Catholic Church. May this unity support you — not only to achieve your own salvation and that of your neighbours but also to maintain this spiritual profile that decides our national identity, our presence in European history and our contribution to the struggle for peace, justice and freedom.

I will repeat here the wish I expressed on 16 May, when addressing more than six thousand Poles during a special audience in Rome:

> At this exceptional meeting today we must hope – with the help of God's grace and through the intercession of Mary Mother of the Church, who is Our Lady of Jasna Góra, Queen of Poland, with the intercession of Saint Stanislaus, Saint Wojciech (Adalbert) and all the Polish saints and blesseds up to Blessed Maximilian Kolbe and Blessed Mary Teresa Ledochowska – that all of us, wherever we may be, may succeed in bearing witness to the maturity of Poland, in strengthening our right of citizenship among all the nations of Europe and of the world, and, in serving this noble purpose, to bear witness to Christian universalism.

That is my heartfelt wish for you and in this spirit I bless you all, as well as your families, your pastors, priests, and the whole Polonia.

"It is from Poland that you have brought over your faith."

Address to the Irish bishops, Dublin

My dear brothers,

1.   Once again I want you to know how profoundly grateful I am to you for your invitation to come to Ireland. For me this visit is the fulfilment of a deep desire of my heart: to come as a servant of the Gospel and as a pilgrim to the Shrine of Our Lady at Knock, on the occasion of its centenary.

I come also as your brother bishop from Rome, and I have greatly looked forward to this day: so that we may celebrate together the unity of the episcopate of Our Lord Jesus Christ, so that we may give public expression to a dimension of our episcopal collegiality, and so that we may reflect together on the rôle of pastoral leadership in the Church, particularly in regard to our own common responsibility for the well-being of the People of God in Ireland.

We are deeply conscious of the special charge that has been laid upon us as bishops. For "by virtue of sacramental consecration and by hierarchical communion" *(Lumen Gentium,* 22) we are constituted members of the college charged with the pastoral mission of Our Lord Jesus Christ.

2.   The episcopal collegiality in which we share is manifested in different ways. Today it is expressed in a very important way: the successor of Peter is present with you, in order personally to confirm you in your faith and apostolic ministry, and, together with you, to exercise the pastoral care of the faithful in Ireland. Thus, my pilgrimage as pastor of the universal Church is seen in its deep dimension of ecclesial and hierarchical communion. And through the action of the Holy Spirit the teaching on collegiality finds expression and actuation here and now.

In my first discourse to the College of Cardinals and to the world after my election to the See of Peter, I urged "a deeper reflection on the implications of the collegial bond" (17 October 1978). I am also convinced that my meeting with the Episcopal Conference today leads to a better understanding of the nature of the Church, viewed as the People of God, "which takes its citizens from every race, making them citizens of a kingdom which is of a heavenly and not an earthly nature" *(Lumen Gentium,* 13).

In our present meeting, we are living the experience of the People of God in Ireland, first in the "vertical" dimension, climbing up, as it were, through all the generations to the very beginnings of Christianity here. At the same time we are mindful of the "horizonal" dimension, realising how the People of God in Ireland are joined in the unity and the universality of the Church with all peoples on the earth, how they share in the mystery of the universal Church and in her great mission of salvation. The bishops of Ireland have, moreover, their own sharing in this dimension of the life of the whole Church because they share in the tasks of the College of Bishops: *cum Petro et sub Petro.* Hence this meeting of the Pope and the bishops of Ireland is highly important and marvellously eloquent, for Ireland and for the universal Church.

3.   The basis of our personal identity, of our common bond and of our ministry is found in Jesus Christ, the Son of God and High Priest of the New Testament. For this reason, brethren, my first exhortation as I come among you today is this: "Let us keep our eyes fixed on Jesus, who inspires and perfects our faith" (Heb 12:2). Since

we are pastors of this flock, we must indeed look to him who is the chief Shepherd — *Princeps Pastorum* (1 Pet 5:4) — to enlighten us, to sustain us, and to give us joy as we serve the flock, leading it "in paths of righteousness for his name's sake" (Ps 23:3).

But the effectiveness of our service to Ireland and to the whole Church is linked with our *personal relationship to him* whom Saint Peter also called "the Shepherd and Bishop of your souls" (1 Pet 2:25). The secure basis for our pastoral leadership is then a deep personal relationship of faith and love with Jesus Christ, our Lord. Like the Twelve, we too were appointed to be with him, to be his companions (cf Mk 3:14). We can present ourselves as religious leaders of our people in the situations that deeply affect their daily lives only after we have been in prayerful communion with the Teacher, only after we have discovered in faith that God has made Christ to be "our wisdom, our righteousness and sanctification and redemption" (1 Cor 1:30). In our own lives we are called to *hear* and *guard* and *do* the word of God. In the sacred scriptures, and especially in the Gospels, we meet Christ constantly; and through the power of the Holy Spirit his words become light and strength for us and for our people. His words themselves contain a power for conversion, and we learn by his example.

Through prayerful contact with the Jesus of the Gospels, we, his servants and apostles, increasingly absorb his serenity and we assume his attitudes. Above all we take on that fundamental attitude of love for his Father, so much so that each one of us finds deep joy and fulfilment in the truth of our filial relationship: *Diligo Patrem* (Jn 14:31) — *Pater diligit Filium* (Jn 3:35). Our relationship with Christ and in Christ finds its supreme and unique expression in the Eucharistic sacrifice, in which we act to the full: *in persona Christi.*

Our personal relationship with Jesus is then a guarantee of confidence for us and for our minstry. In our faith we find the victory that overcomes the world. Because we are united with Jesus and sustained by him, there is no challenge we cannot meet, no difficulty we cannot sustain, no obstacle we cannot overcome for the Gospel. Indeed, Christ himself guarantees that "he who believes in me will also do the works that I do; and greater works than these will he do . . ." (Jn 14:12). Yes, brethren, the answer to so many problems is found only in faith — a faith manifested and sustained in prayer.

4.   Our relationship with Jesus will be the fruitful basis of our relationship with our priests, as we strive to be their brother, father, friend and guide. In the charity of Christ we are called to listen to and to understand them; to exchange views regarding evangelisation and the pastoral mission they share with us as co-workers with the Order of Bishops. For the entire Church — but especially for the priests — we must be a human sign of the love of Christ and the fidelity of the Church. Thus we sustain our priests with the Gospel message, supporting them by the certainty of the Magisterium, and fortifying them against the pressures that they must resist. By word and example we must constantly invite our priests to prayer.

We are called to show generously to our priests that human concern, personal interest and sincere esteem whereby they will readily perceive our love. Despite the multiplicity of our commitments, our priests must recognise in us the faithful reflection of the shepherd and bishop of their souls (cf 1 Pet 2:25).

Our priests have made many sacrifices, including the renunciation of marriage for the sake of the kingdom of heaven; and they must be firmly encouraged to persevere. Fidelity to Christ and the demands of human dignity and freedom require them to maintain constancy in their commitment.

The pastoral solicitude we have for priests must also be shown to our seminarists.

Let us exercise personally also our responsibility for their training in the word of God, and for all the formation they receive in Ireland and abroad, including Rome. In my letter to the bishops of the Church on Holy Thursday I wrote: "The full reconstitution of the life of the seminaries throughout the Church will be the best proof of the achievment of the renewal to which the Council directed the Church."

5.   Like Christ, the bishop comes among the laity as one who serves. The laity are the vast majority of the flock of Jesus Christ. Through baptism and confirmation, Christ himself gives them a sharing in his own mission of salvation. Together with the clergy and the religious, the laity make up the one communion of the Church: "a chosen race, a royal priesthood, a holy nation, God's own people" (1 Pet 2:9).

The greatest expression of the bishop's service to the laity is his personal proclamation of the word of God, which reaches its summit in the Eucharist (cf *Presbyterorum Ordinis,* 5). As a faithful steward of the Gospel message, each bishop is called to expound to his people "the whole mystery of Christ" (*Christus Dominus,* 12).

As the bishop proclaims the dignity of the laity, it is also his rôle to do everything possible to promote their contribution to evangelisation, urging them to assume every responsibility that is theirs in temporal realities. In the words of Paul VI, "Their own field of evangelising activity is the vast and complicated world of politics, society and economics, the world of culture, of the sciences and the arts, of international life, of mass media" (*Evangelii Nuntiandi,* 70). And there are other spheres of activity in which they can effectively work for the transformation of society.

In accordance with the will of God, the Christian family is an evangelising agent of immense importance. In all the moral issues of authentic Christian living, the laity look to the bishops as their leaders, their pastors and their fathers. The bishops must constantly reply to the great cry of humanity, usually not articulated in words, but very

"Today, you must keep the city and the factory for God . . ."

real: "We wish to see Jesus" (Jn 12:21). And in this the bishops have a rôle of great importance: to show Jesus to the world; to present him authentically and convincingly: Jesus Christ, true God and true man — Jesus Christ, the way and the truth and the life — Jesus Christ the man of prayer.

6. Bishops are called to be true fathers of all their people, excelling in the spirit of love and solicitude for all (cf *Christus Dominus,* 16). They should have a special care for those who live on the margin of society. Among those most needing pastoral care from bishops are prisoners. My dear brothers, do not neglect to provide for their spiritual needs and to concern yourselves also about their material conditions and their families.

Try to bring the prisoners such spiritual care and guidance as may help to turn them from the ways of violence and crime, and make their detention instead be an occasion of true conversion to Christ and personal experience of love. Have a special care for young offenders. So often their wayward lives are due to society's neglect more than to their own sinfulness. Detention should be especially for them a school of rehabilitation.

7. In the light of our commitment to Jesus, and to his Gospel, in the light also of our collegial responsibility, our meeting here today assumes a special importance because of the present difficult time for Ireland, on account of the whole situation relating to Northern Ireland. These circumstances impelled some people to advise me against making a pilgrimage to Ireland. These very difficulties, however, make it all the more important to be here, to share closely with all of you these uncommon trials, and to seek in union with you the aid of God and good human counsel. These reasons for coming here gain in eloquence if they are placed in the framework of my visit to the

United Nations, where it will be my privilege and duty to seek out ways of living in peace and reconciliation throughout the world.

I am sure that the pastors of the Church in Ireland have a better understanding and deeper feeling for the painful problems of the present moment. Their duty, as I pointed out already, is to guide and sustain the flock, the People of God, but they can perform this duty in no other way than by suffering with those who suffer, and by weeping with those who weep (cf Rom 12:15).

On this point, I draw my conviction both from the Gospel and from the personal and historical experience that I had in the Church and nation from which I come. During the last two centuries, the Church in Poland has struck root in a special way in the soul of the nation. Part of the reason for this is that its pastors — its bishops and priests — did not hesitate to share in the trials and sufferings of their fellow countrymen. They were found among those deported to Siberia in the time of the Czars. They were found in the concentration camps at the time of the unleashing of Nazi terrorism during the last war. This self-sacrifice and dedication confirmed more fully the truth about the priest, that he is "chosen from among men . . . to act on behalf of men" (Heb 5:1).

8.   Because of this faithfulness to their brothers and sisters, to their fellow countrymen, the sons and daughters of the same homeland, pastors, and especially bishops, must reflect beforehand on how to prevent bloodshed, hatred and terror, on how to strengthen peace, and on how to spare the people from these terrible sufferings. This was the message that Paul VI repeated over thirty times, in appealing for peace and justice in relation to Northern Ireland. He never ceased to condemn violence and to appeal for justice. "We earnestly beg" — he wrote to Cardinal Conway on the solemnity of Pentecost 1974 —

> that all violence should cease, from whatever side it may come, for it is contrary to the law of God and to the Christian and civilised way of life; that, in response to the common Christian conscience and the voice of reason, a climate of mutual trust and dialogue be re-established in justice and charity; that the real deep-seated causes of social unrest – which are not to be reduced to differences of a religious nature – be identified and eliminated.

These efforts, venerable and dear brothers, must be continued. Faith and social ethics demand from us respect for the established State authorities. But this respect also finds its expression in individual acts of mediation, in persuasion, in moral influence, and indeed in firm requests. For while it is true, as Saint Paul says, that he who is in authority bears the sword (cf Rom 13:4), which we renounce in accordance with the clear recommendation of Christ to Peter in the Garden of Gethsemane (cf Mt 26:52), nevertheless, precisely because we are defenceless, we have a special right and duty to influence those who wield the sword of authority. For it is well known that in the field of political action, as elsewhere, not everything can be obtained by means of the sword. There are deeper reasons and stronger laws to which men, nations and peoples are subject. It is for us to discern these reasons and in their light to become, before those in authority, spokesmen for the moral order. This order is superior to force and violence. In this superiority of the moral order is expressed all the dignity of men and nations.

9.   I recall with deep satisfaction a significant feature in the series of events connected with my journey to Ireland. It is highly significant that the invitation from the episcopate, through its four archbishops, was followed by invitations from other Churches,

especially from Irish Anglicans. I take the opportunity to stress this once again and to express my renewed thanks and appreciation to them. I see in this circumstance a very promising sign of hope. In view of the reasons with which you are all familiar, I have been unable to accept this truly ecumenical invitation by visiting Armagh in Northern Ireland, and have been able to go no further than Drogheda. Nonetheless, the eloquence of this ecumenical readiness fully corresponds to what was expressed in my first encyclical:

> In the present historical situation of Christianity and the world, the only possibility we see of fulfilling the Church's universal mission, with regard to ecumenical questions, is that of seeking sincerely, perseveringly, humbly and also courageously the ways of drawing closer and of union . . . We must seek unity without being discouraged at the difficulties that can appear or accumulate along that road; otherwise we would be unfaithful to the word of Christ, we would fail to accomplish his testament. Have we the right to run this risk? (*Redemptor Hominis*, 6).

The witness to faith in Christ which we share with our brethren must continue to find expression not only in prayer for full unity but also in prayer and sustained effort for reconciliation and peace in this beloved land. This union of endeavour must lead us to take into consideration the whole mechanism of strife, cruelty, and growing hatred, in order to "overcome evil with good" (Rom 12:12).

What are we to do? I earnestly hope that, in a continued effort, you and our brothers in the faith will become spokesmen for the just reasons of peace and reconciliation before those who wield the sword and those who perish by the sword. How sad it is to think of all the lives that have been lost, especially the lives of young people. What a terrible loss for their country, for the Church, for the whole of humanity!

10.   Venerable pastors of the Church in Ireland: this service to justice and social love that is yours to perform in this present moment is difficult. It is difficult, but it is your duty! Do not fear: Christ is with you! He will give you his Holy Spirit: the Spirit of counsel and fortitude. And although this Spirit of God is frequently resisted, in the heart of man and in the history of humanity, by "the spirit of this world" and by "the spirit of darkness", nevertheless the final victory can only be that of love and truth. Continue steadfast in the difficult service that is yours, doing everything "in the name of the Lord Jesus" (Col 3:17). Be assured that in your ministry you have my support and that of the universal Church. And all men and women of goodwill stand by you in the quest for peace, justice and human dignity.

Dear brothers, in the name of Jesus Christ and his Church I thank you — and through you, all Ireland. I thank you for your fidelity to the Gospel, for your everlasting contribution to the spread of the Catholic faith, for your authentic and irreplaceable service to the world.

As far as the future goes, brethren, courage and trust!

Walk in the illumination of the paschal mystery — in that light which must never be extinguished in your land! Go forward in the power of the Holy Spirit, in the merits of Jesus Christ!

And rejoice with a great joy in the unfailing intercession and protection of Mary, Great Mary, Mother of God, Queen of the Apostles, Queen of Ireland, Queen of Peace!

Brethren, let us go forward together, for the good of Ireland and for the glory of the Most Holy Trinity. And therefore "Let us keep our eyes fixed on Jesus, who inspires and perfects our faith."

"Slán!"

"The time has come for me to leave Ireland."

Address on departure from Shannon Airport

Your Excellency, Mr President of Ireland;
Your Eminence, Cardinal Primate of all Ireland.
Dear brothers and sisters,

The time has come for me to leave Ireland, to continue my pastoral mission, my apostolic journey.

I came here to proclaim peace and love, to speak to you about the Son of God made man, about your life in Christ. Yes, as successor of the Apostle Peter I came to confirm my brethren in the faith, and to ask all Ireland to lift up its heart to a new vision of hope — in the words of Saint Paul: to "Christ Jesus our hope" (1 Tim 1:1).

I began my pilgrimage under the protection of Our Blessed Lady, and on the feast of the Archangels. And I take leave of you on the feast of Theresa of the Child Jesus, spendid example of joyful simplicity, and proof of the extraordinary effectiveness of generous Christian love.

I am deeply grateful for all the kindnesses shown me by the civil and religious authorities of this land. I also thank those who worked so hard and with such great skill here in Ireland to organise the many details of this visit. I thank all the people for the warm and loving reception in which they manifested their keen sense of humanity and their lively faith.

With the Apostle Paul, I now beg you for ever "to lead a life worthy of the calling to which you have been called . . . eager to maintain the unity of the Spirit in the bond of peace" (Eph 4:1, 3).

In the name of the Lord I exhort you to preserve the great treasure of your fidelity to Jesus Christ and to his Church. Like the early Christian community described in the Acts of the Apostles, Ireland is called to be "faithful to the teaching of the apostles, to the brotherhood, to the breaking of bread and to the prayers" (Acts 2:42).

Ireland: *semper fidelis,* always faithful!

Ireland: always faithful!

Moladh go deo le Dia!